Presbyterians on the Frontier:
A Story of
Presbyterian Border Ministry
1984 to 2014

ISBN 978-0-9817976-1-8

Published by Just Trade Center

http://www.presbyteriansonthefrontier.net

You may order this book in print through Available from Amazon.com, CreateSpace.com, and other retail outlets or by contacting the author at parrish@parrishjones.net. An eBook is also available for Kindle and other devices.

Presbyterians on the Frontier:

A Story of

Presbyterian Border Ministry

1984 to 2014

By Parrish W. Jones, Ph.D.

I dedicate this work to the many persons, Mexican and U.S., who have served on the staffs, the boards and as mission volunteers over the last 30 years and to those who have sacrificed to volunteer time, talents and treasure to the work of Presbyterian Border Ministry. However, it would be an error not to dedicate it also to the hundreds and thousands who may serve in similar ways over the next 30 years. Without a doubt we must place the book in the hands of God whose blessings live in and through us all.

Contents

Acknowledgements

I have many persons I need to thank for making this book possible.

First and foremost has to be Mark Adams who encouraged me from the first time I mentioned the idea and who has promoted the work.

Those persons who made donations on the bet I'd complete the work and gave me donations with only a promise of a signed copy of the book. Without their generosity and trust I could not have completed the work.

I cannot begin to list all the persons with whom I held interviews and received hospitality. I received the hospitality of many who gave me a space to stay and asked nothing in return: Mr. and Mrs. Roberto Armendariz, Rev. and Mrs. Juan Pablo Gutiérrez and their family, Mr. and Mrs. Lee Van Hamm, Mr. and Mrs. David Thomas, and Mr. and Mrs. Jesús Gallegos.

I received translation assistance for the interviews from Jocabed Gallegos and Josias Casanova.

Several readers and editors have helped perfect the manuscript: Bob Battenfield, David Thomas, Genie and Hector Zavaleta, Mark Adams, and Elizabeth Spender. Each made a significant contribution to improving the completed work.

Thanks to my daughter, Celese Jones, created the front cover for the work.

Abbreviations

BPM   Baja Presbyterian Missions-San Diego, CA
CeM   Compañeros en Misión, Nogales, AZ and Nogales, Sonora, MX
DHS   Department of Homeland Security
FdC   Frontera De Cristo, Douglas, AZ and Agua Prieta, Sonora, MX
ICE   Immigration and Customs Enforcement
INPM   National Presbyterian Church of México (Iglesia Nacional Presbiteriana de México)
INS   Immigration and Naturalization Service
JCM   Joint Commission on Mission
MRC   Migrant Resource Center, Agua Prieta, Sonora, MX
PA   Proyecto Amistad, Laredo, TX and Nuevo Laredo, Tamaulipas, MX
PBM   Presbyterian Border Ministry
PdF   Pasos de Fe, El Paso, TX and Ciudad Juárez, Chihuahua, MX
PdC   Puentes de Cristo, McAllen, TX and Reynosa, Tamaulipas, MX
PH   Pueblos Hermanos, SanDiego, CA and Tijuana, Baja, MX
YAV   Young Adult Volunteer

NOTE: Above I give the names of the cities where the ministry is located for purposes of administration. In several cases the ministries extend far into the Mexican nation.

In Memory of Saúl Tijerina

May 3, 1925 to January 15, 2002

"The National Presbyterian Church of México dreams of having a very real presence on the border, with established and self-sustaining churches. It would like to see those established churches on the border, in partnership with the U.S. Presbyterian church, respond to the pain the border causes, the damage it does to family, the vices it promotes:

Dr. Tijerina in fields with Migrant

unemployment, illness, the exploitation of women in the twin plants, and lack of concern for the family's well-being. The constantly-changing border population and the pain and sorrow of its people are, and will continue to be, a priority concern for the church - as they are to God and rightly so." —Saúl Tijerina as found in "Talking Points 25 for 25th", PCUSA.

When I first began researching for the following book, I kept encountering the name Saúl Tijerina. Then when I began interviewing I kept hearing his name. It was clear to anyone who had worked in Presbyterian Border Ministry (PBM) and in the Iglesia Presbiteriana

Nacional de México (INPM) in the northern part of México, Dr. Tijerina was a significant figure whose impact spread over the whole region.

His stature was not limited to the north but impacted the whole of the INPM and México. He served numerous terms as moderator of the General Assembly of the INPM, a position far more influential in the INPM than it is in the PCUSA. He also served as the Rector of the Presbyterian Theological Seminary of México in México City for eight years (1975 to 1982). Before promoting and participating in the founding of PBM, he helped to establish a college and a seminary in the city of Monterrey where he served twenty years as pastor of the church "El Buen Pastor" where he had received nurture as an adolescent and during his studies in Seminary.

As a pastor, he nurtured others who would become leaders in the INPM and in the UPCUSA and the PCUS and in their successor denomination the PCUSA. He was known as a consummate pastor and teacher and also for his political capacity to navigate denominational waters. Jerry Stacy, first U.S. Coordinator of PBM, said of him, "He understood the Mexican church and the U.S. church as well as anyone and helped us all understand the importance of the work along the border. He gained your confidence immediately."

Dr. Tijerina came from the most unlikely place to his role as national and international leader. Born in Refugio (Refuge or Sanctuary), a small village near Monterrey, México to a poor family as the next to the youngest of twelve children, he was nurtured in the Presbyterian Church his father loved. As a peasant farmer, his father earned little income, but what he lacked in riches, he made up for in hope for his children. Recognizing Saúl's academic possibilities, he arranged for him to continue his education in Monterrey once he had completed the fifth grade—the final grade of school in his village.

In Monterrey, Saúl was nurtured by the pastor of the El Buen Pastor Church where he would one day become pastor. Once Saúl completed his secondary education, he went on to the Presbyterian Seminary in Coyoacán where he was able to begin working in ministries around the city. On school breaks he returned home to assist in the ministries in his community. Under the guidance of respected pastors and gifted by God, he developed into a man of uncommon wisdom.

His younger brother, Edwin, reported, "Despite being the next to youngest in our family, all our brothers and sisters consulted with Saúl on any major decision. He was as loved and respected in the family as he was in the church."

His colleagues, Jerry Stacy and Hector Zavaleta, testify that Saúl worked with uncanny insight and grace to bring understanding and cooperation between the Mexican Presbyterian Church and the Presbyterian Churches of the U.S. Then he worked with wisdom and energy to lead to the establishment of PBM. He held the vision of a binational mutual mission work together as he helped navigate and overcome the cultural differences that hindered cooperation. His deep and profound understanding of scripture helped the Joint Commission on Mission understand how to base Presbyterian Border Ministry in the Word of God.

(I give thanks to Hector and Genie Zavaleta, whom I interviewed In Tucson in June, 2013, and who helped gather the majority of the information and documents used for this memorial.)

Preface

One Sunday morning in June, 1991 I began an odyssey with my family while preparing myself for worship. My daughter, Kimberly, called and recounted with excitement what she was doing and the things she was seeing on her high school mission trip to Arizona. She had visited Guadalupe, a native American village now surrounded by the sprawling suburbs of Phoenix, and the growing city of Agua Prieta four hours south in Sonora, MX. In Agua Prieta she had learned about Presbyterian Border Ministry, met the co-coordinators, and learned that there was a program for college students called Young Adult Volunteers in the Presbyterian Church. With excitement she asked, "Dad, do you think I could be a YAV next summer and see if I can get placed in Agua Prieta?"

I told her we could certainly talk about it and that I would do some research to learn more. As hard as it is to believe, the internet was barely functional at that time. The church had almost nothing available via electronic media and while I was as up to date as anyone in using the newest technology, e-mail and the like was cumbersome and unreliable. But I kept my promise.

As important, her question got me to thinking. I had accumulated four weeks of continuing education and when January came I would receive two more. With the time came some money. In savings already there was about $800. In January that would grow to $1,200. I had no plans. I was tired of attending conferences and had no desire to spend time on a seminary campus. The money was not enough to do any kind of extensive sabbatical. Kimberly's question raised the issue, "Could my family go on a mission together?"

After worship, I talked with Mary Ellen, and our two children still living at home, Jason and Christy, about the possibility of going to the border the next summer. The idea was exciting to them. The next week I contacted a few people to learn more about PBM and the YAV program. Then I contacted the U.S. co-coordinator of FdC to see if he was open to us coming, what kind of living arrangements there may be, and what kind of work we could do.

Kimberly was accepted into the YAV program for the next summer after she finished her first year in college. Mary Ellen and I took a year of Spanish language at the University of Pittsburgh at Johnstown where I taught philosophy part time while she was studying sociology and anthropology. We made plans and, as we did so, our church became excited about the prospects of this adventure.

The session (governing board of a Presbyterian Church) agreed to give me eight weeks—six of continuing education and two of vacation. It also planned how to deal with pastoral care and worship in my absence. Lay persons in the church were recruited to preach to avoid honorariums except on communion Sundays. A retired minister agreed to observe communion with the church to eliminate the need of honorariums. Mary Ellen asked for and received a leave of absence from the hospital where she worked.

And so, we were off on our baptism into mission—Mary Ellen, Jason and Christy and I to Agua Prieta—on Pentecost Sunday after being commissioned by and celebrating communion with our church. Jason and Christy said we looked a lot like the Beverly Hillbillies in our mini van with tortoise shell carrier on top and four bikes hanging off the back. But off we were for what was our first cross country adventure together. With some disappointment, Kimberly was assigned to Pueblos Hermanos in Tijuana.

After a few stops to see places of historic importance and natural beauty along the way, we arrived at the mission house in Douglas, AZ where we were greeted by Les and Kathy Winters. They showed us to the section of the house we would call home for a little more than six weeks. We settled in.

The next six weeks we made friends with the Jésus "Chuy" Gallegos Viesca family, the Mexican co-coordinator and his family, with whom we remain close. We also made friends with folk on both sides of the border whose friendship and love we still enjoy. From then to now those relationships have grown and deepened.

We also became immersed in a new idea of mission that was struggling for expression and effectiveness, a vision that originated in the hearts and minds of the leadership of the National Presbyterian Church of México (INPM) under the guidance of Pastor Dr. Saúl Tijerina. That vision was for a truly binational and mutual mission venture that would overcome the old paternalistic model of mission that led the INPM to request that U.S. Presbyterians recall their missionaries two decades earlier. (See Part I)

I spent hours in conversation with Les and others about the mission work and its struggles. For a lot of reasons Frontera de Cristo (FdC) and the small church in Agua Prieta were struggling. When we left to return home later that summer, we did so with great sadness and with the fear that neither FdC nor the church would still exist in a couple of years. Twenty-four years later both are doing well and, in Agua Prieta, there is another church and a nice community center that provides a number of services to the communities surrounding it.

That summer I attended several board meetings of FdC where the difficulties of binational ministry manifested themselves— linguistic, cultural, theological, and missional. Despite agreement on the goals of bi-nationality and mutuality, the old habits of paternalism continued to plague conversations.

Mexicans tended to defer to the folks with the money —the U.S. Presbyterians. The more organized and analytic approach to planning of U..S. Presbyterians tended to trump the not so well organized ambitions and planned desires and dreams of the Mexicans. As the Rev. Jesús Gallegos told me a few years later, "The Americans want us to bring them a well developed plan of action with statements about goals, plans for accomplishing the goals, where the money will come from and what the outcomes should be. We don't think that way. We have an idea, get excited about it, and just sort of know it will work. By the time we are finished trying to convince the Americans, we are discouraged. There's always this cultural difference getting in our way. It's not a matter of good or bad. It's a matter of difference. Because most of the money comes from the U.S., we feel we have to submit. Marriage isn't easy. This is harder."

Two years later I tried to get some of the folks from my church to travel with me to visit FdC and learn. I was unsuccessful, so I went alone. By this trip the site in Nogales was up and running, so after spending almost a week in Agua Prieta, I also traveled to Nogales. I learned about near miracles taking place in both places. A lot of progress was made in new directions with FdC and astounding and exciting accomplishments in Nogales.

I wondered how to proceed. My presbytery, the Presbytery of Redstone, was involved in trying to start a mission venture in Egypt. I joined the mission committee and discovered that the project was facing three daunting problems:

First, communications were limping along. Every letter to Egypt took months to receive a response. The lack of communication seemed to bode poorly for the project. Even determining a time for a visit seemed nearly impossible. Telephone communications were archaic at that time in less developed countries so one did not just pick up a phone.

Second, money stood in the way. Our presbytery was located in the rust belt and the hardest hit part of it. The people of Redstone, even the better off ones, were not very well off. The churches were struggling to make ends meet and so was the presbytery. How many of us could afford the nearly $2,000 in travel expenses much less do anything of consequence?

Three, it seemed the Egyptian partners were disinterested in the direction our presbytery wanted to go which may have accounted for the lack of responsiveness from them.

I suggested that, should the committee agree, we could open talks with FdC not in place of but in addition to Egypt. Also, the General Assembly had declared 1996 to be "Year in Mission with Latin America." Redstone could participate in that emphasis by doing a mission that year and do so at far less expense. The committee agreed and asked that I work with another member on the idea.

We went to work and developed a plan to have a small group go to FdC in the spring to explore with the FdC board the possibility of a mission relationship. Assuming a plan could be developed we went ahead with a plan for a large intergenerational group to go in June. The committee adopted the plan and agreed to fund it with scholarships, the registration fees for FdC, and some expenses for materials. Preparing the first group was a challenge as I had never done such a thing and neither had my colleague. I drew on my experiences and reflections from our summer in mission. I prepared Bible reflections and studies for the members, talked about mutual mission and collected resources to help us deal with cultural sensitivity and and spirituality.

The results were incredible in terms of our spirit and sense of cohesion. However, the problem of point of view persisted. I heard quite often statements that said, "I want to help those who are less well off than me." "It's so sad to see people living in such misery." "It seems we could do more to help 'them'." No matter how often I responded that one of the things we needed to do was seek ways in which the Mexican Presbyterians could help us, similar paternalistic ideas or pity continued to surface. Were there ways we could see ourselves as the less fortunate? In what ways are we "the least of these"?

No matter how much energy we put into changing the focus, the focus never fully changed. Several of our adults and young people went year after year on these mission trips. Some caught on. Others filled out their application for participation each year giving as their reason for wanting to go, "I feel called to help the less fortunate." The Spirit eventually helps others to see themselves as going on a spiritual journey of relationship with brothers and sisters. Some of those relationships continue today via e-mail and Facebook.

There were many victories, but changing the way a dominant culture thinks about itself is not easy, but with God's help some of us caught the vision quite well. All of us find ourselves having to work hard at not losing sight of who we are in relationship to persons who are materially poorer but still wealthy in respects long relationships help us discover.

I can say that I am richer today than I was in 1992. That new wealth comes from the many conversion experiences I have had because I have been engaged in mission in México and Colombia. I have learned not to presume that I know much at all about the complexity of life on the border and every time I go, I come home newly enriched by the experience.

Because of my immersion experiences at the border, I have become close friends with several migrant families who have come to live at the border because of economic distress. They have made a life there and stabilized. The experiences there and my improving Spanish have opened doors to share with migrants in the U.S., some of whom are here legally and others who are here undocumented. Their stories have transformed my understanding of myself which has transformed my understanding of persons who have been displaced.

All of these experiences have led me to value the vision of mission that led to the founding of Presbyterian Border Ministry. Today, in the PCUSA our mission energy is motivated almost as a whole by the requests of our mission partners instead of our desires. Because of our cultural tendencies, we still find U.S. Presbyterians going to other countries, seeing something they think the people living in the region need, and providing it with little or no sensitivity to the viewpoint of our partners. The challenge of PBM was to make sure that both partners listened to each other and honored each other's points of view.

When I first started in mission work, our focus was doing work: building this, repairing that, painting the inside or outside of a church, and so on. This focus took our eyes off of relationship. Today, mission is understood as principally about relationships. PBM has helped transform our sense of mission from "doing for" to "doing with", or more importantly, being with our brothers and sisters in Christ. We call it accompaniment, a strange word to us but a common one for Spanish speakers as they consistently ask, "Do you want me to accompany you?" "Will you accompany me?" "How many do you need to accompany you in this or that?" The word can mean everything from "walk with", "travel with", "work with", or "help". We translate their words to "You want me to go with you." Perhaps, you can see the deeper meaning in the Spanish manner of speaking.

This new way is transformative and affirms the dignity of others. However, just as it took Peter and the other Apostles a great struggle of faith and theological mind set, PBM has struggled as the narrative will show with how exactly these various cultures can be truly engaged in complete mutuality. In fact, the transformations are continuous as new persons become engaged and struggle with their cultural bias. It has gone both ways, but I have witnessed the struggle the most in the U.S. as we gathered to study, pray, learn and delegation build.

When our trips turned from building, improving and repairing things to relationship building, learning, and cultural immersion, one elder, a sincere and gifted man, told me he did not wish to go anymore. "I'm not into the head stuff. I just want to do." That was his sense of giftedness. He was that way at home. Already in his 1970s, his contribution to the church was fixing and repairing whether it be the church or the homes of his brothers and sisters in Christ, but our partners were not in need of work projects. They were in need of relationship and understanding. They needed compassion not pity.

These Christians are struggling with the issue at root. As I write, my ears ring with the words of an elder who asked me when I prepared to take another mission trip, "What are you going to do?" I responded, "I'm going to learn about what they are doing, to build relationships, and lend encouragement." "Why don't you just send them the money, won't that help them more?"

This was not said in rancor but in concern. The reality is that we can send money, but PBM has taught us, as has the mission work in so many places, that our partners want our presence and all the money in the world does not give that. I never return to Agua Prieta that someone doesn't say, "Thank you for coming back. So many come and we never see them again." My brothers and sisters in Colombia, where I spent the year of 2007 teaching theology at the Reformed university, are always asking, "When will you be back?" I wish I knew.

Faithful relationships we learn from scripture are what being Christian is all about. PBM has been and remains a cauldron for building faithful relationships of true covenant between the presbyterians to the north and those to the south. It has taught me a great deal. I have learned, grown, been transformed. Through my work I have received new vision that is constantly being renewed.

My prayer is that through this book, I may convey that transforming vision in such a way that those who read receive a new vision. That is what I understand conversion to be—

> offer your bodies as a living sacrifice, holy and pleasing to God—this is your true and proper worship. Do not conform to the pattern of this world, but be transformed by the renewing of your mind. Then you will be able to test and approve what God's will is—his good, pleasing and perfect will. (Romans 12:1-

Introduction

México demands our attention in the U.S. because we are geographically joined at the hip forming the appearance of a bent over human. Using your imagination, if Maine is the head, and Texas, New México, Arizona and California the pelvis and rump, México is the legs. It is impossible to imagine two nations so close geographically not having a necessary relationship: economically, politically, socially, culturally, and ecclesiastically. Indeed, the two countries do have

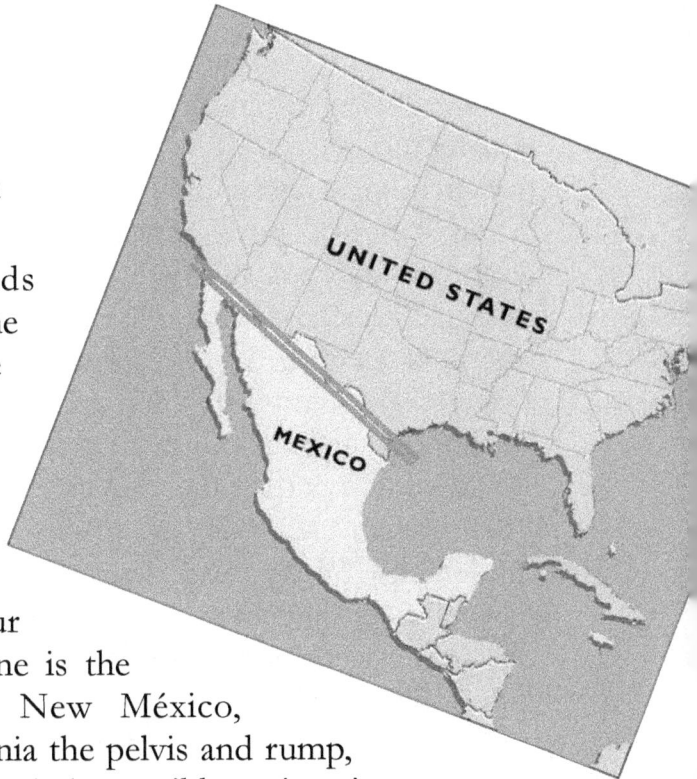

both strong relationships through which we share in important hemispheric work, drug abatement, economic development and social, educational and artistic enrichment. We also have threatening relationships through which the U.S. imposes, often with Mexican political and economic complicity, economic and political activity on México that benefits the U.S but most often hurts millions of Mexican peasants and industrial and corporate workers.

México never emerged completely from the legacy of colonialism. Unlike the U.S. whose system developed out of an imaginative and strong middle class almost from its beginning, Latin American nations were almost all subjected to aristocratic government following independence from Spain. In México, as in most of Latin America, no significant middle class of business entrepreneurs developed until very recently. Post-colonial México continued to be mired in the excesses of the degenerating Aristocratic lifestyle, the ownership of large estates (latifundia) and great wealth by the ecclesial authorities, and the consequent poverty of the masses.

México was the object of extractive colonialism from the first invasion of its shores by Spain under the leadership of Hérnan Cortez in 1519, a conquest virtually completed two years later in 1521. Its massive resources were mined and its wealth returned to Spain until 1821 when it was given its independence. Political independence does not mean economic independence because the Mexican Aristocracy of Spanish descent became its rulers. Like their predecessors, their lives were marked by luxuriant excess funded by cheap labor, abundant natural resources, and easy access to all the comforts of life from Europe and the U.S. Development of national infrastructure and industry was of no concern until the late 19th and early 20th century when the revolutionary movement from below[1] picked up energy from mass movements of workers and peasants.

In 1860, Benito Juárez, a full blooded indigenous person and lawyer, amassed an army, successfully attacked México City and became president. Proceeding with liberal reforms including freedom of speech, land reform, ecclesiastical restrictions, and the suspension of foreign debt, his tenure lasted but a brief time before France intervened and appointed Maximilian I emperor of México. Maximilian I survived until 1867 when the army of Benito Juárez captured and executed him and once more claimed power.

Having regained power, Juárez pushed his anti-ecclesial reforms in the form of religious liberty that opened the doors for Protestant mission work. The U.S. Presbyterian Churches, among others, began work in México in 1872 when the Northern Presbyterian Church, known as the PCUSA, sent missionaries. Its reasons for doing so are instructive:
The 35th Annual Report (1872) of the PCUSA[2] Board of Foreign Missions gives five reasons:

1. The great promise. In further support of the facts already stated, it may be said that after the

---

[1] The term "from below" is an indication of the type of revolution. Instead of being a Middle Class led revolution such as in the American Colonies, many developing world revolutions began from the misery of the poor.

[2] The name and initials of the present PCUSA were chosen by the merger of the UPC and PCUS in 1984 to reclaim the name of the unified church prior to the Civil War.

downfall of the Empire of Maximilian and the Papal Alliances of his usurped throne, a great reaction was produced in the public mind.

2.   The evangelization of Mexico (sic) is geographically and therefore providentially assigned to Protestants of the United States. No other evangelical nation is brought in contact with it. It lies upon our south-western frontier as only a part of our own land.

3. The *whole social, commercial, and political drift of Mexico depends on the establishment of free thought, enlightened patriotism, and sound moral character; and these can only be gained by those same religious truths which have elevated our own and all other Christian nations.*

4. The *purification of the Papacy* itself in Mexico demands the vital, not to say the healthful rivalry of Protestantism.

5. The field is not a difficult one, nor is it far distant. [3]

Apart from the practical possibility and perhaps a true sense of compulsion to evangelize, reasons three and four are clearly paternalistic, if not imperialistic. Reason four lifts up the anti-Catholic nature of the enterprise that remains a legacy in México to this day.

---

3 Thirty Fifth Annual Report (1872), p. 27 as quoted in Hegeman p. 111. Emphasis mine. The document sadly did not adopt the Mexican spelling for their nations which is "México".

Paternalism remains one of the sharpest and most difficult aspects of doing mission with México as it does with all other nations. Paternalistic missions is one of the byproducts of U.S. political relations with all of Latin America.

This fact does not denigrate the faithful commitment and service of many mission workers from the U.S. whose only concern was to share the gospel with the people of México. However, México was clearly seen as "a part of our own land" integrally connected to the U.S. as if an appendage.

Paternalism was not unique to Presbyterians. It was pervasive among Protestants in the U.S. While reason two can reasonably be understood as Christian, the third reason is no more than a European world view we now call humanism, a view of the Enlightenment. Protestants were not only engaging in evangelism but in cultural, economic and political transformation—seeking to remake México in the mold of U.S. political and cultural ideals.

In 1914 another such meeting occurred among U.S. Presbyterian, Methodist and Disciples of Christ Churches in Cincinnati, Ohio. The agencies adopted what they called the Cincinnati Plan which divided México into three regions. The Presbyterians agreed to abandon the north and central regions and work only in southern México and the Yucatán. The churches of the U.S. decided that Calvinists would become Wesleyans and vice versa. In 1916 the international mission agencies (all from Europe and the U.S.) met in Panama City, Panama to consult and establish comity agreements intended to end the impression that the denominations were competing for adherents and to avoid confusion among those they wished to evangelize over these differing expressions of a common faith. The agreements ceded Presbyterians Guatemala in Central America and Chile, Colombia, Venezuela and Argentina in South America.[4] Both these meetings assumed that the churches of Europe and the U.S. were free to dictate to the churches and their leaders in the Caribbean and Latin America without consideration or consultation with the leadership of the indigenous churches. The plan was imposed but not necessarily accepted.

The leaders of the Presbyterian Church in México rejected the plan and established the National Presbyterian Church of México. U.S. Presbyterians quietly accepted this decision but sent mission workers only to the south and Yucatán, abandoning their work in the north. The results were mixed. In the south, the Presbyterian Church strengthened and grew. When Presbyterian Border Ministry was established in 1984, there was hardly a Presbyterian to be found in the north except for a few clustered near Monterrey, Nuevo Leon.[5]

Just prior to these paternalistic decisions, and the reorganization of the churches of México another important political transformation occurred. In 1914, when the Zapatistas of the south—followers of Emiliano Zapata— and the Villistas—followers of Pancho Villa— of the north met in México City, having successfully overthrown the government. As revolutionaries, they had no real understanding of

---

[4] Hegeman, p. 152.

[5] Stacy, Presbyterian Border Ministry, Chapter 1.

governing a nation since they were without the necessary education or experience. Those who stepped in were either newly rich or liberalized Aristocrats. The government changed to a democratic model, imposed anti-clerical/ecclesiastical laws, confiscated church wealth, and the land of much of the legacy of latifundia —the large landholdings of the aristocracy. Land redistribution occurred in many regions of the nation. Sadly, democracy waned in the face of a one party system that retained control until the 1990s. This transformation led to extremely strained relations with the U.S.

The Presbyterian Mission Board had failed to succeed in one area, namely social transformation of the kind it had projected. Free thought and enlightened patriotism had not led to a U.S. style government but to the first radical left revolution in the world, predating that of the 1917 revolution in Russia. Some new thinking was needed in our approaches to missions but little changed for the next fifty to sixty years.

By the time Presbyterian Border Ministry was established, México had progressed economically but poverty was still rampant, life was difficult, and the government had made decisions that proved to be double edged in result. The entrenchment of the wealthy prior to the 1911 Revolution continued and infrastructural and industrial production were ignored. The new government had learned the bad habits of the past—living off the bounty of resources while investing little for a future when the resources would be depleted.

Following the failures of the Green Revolution that promised to transform Mexican agriculture into an economic juggernaut in the 1950s, México tried to change direction. In 1965 México established a one-hundred kilometer wide Free Trade Zone along the U.S./ México border. The U.S. ended the Bracero program which closed many jobs once held by Mexican workers. In this zone U.S. or other international corporations could avoid export taxes if their products never moved out of the zone into other parts of México. Likewise when the resources or products only moved back and forth across the border with the U.S., México charged no tariffs.

In response, U.S. corporations shipped parts and materials manufactured in other places to the U.S. side of the border to be stored in warehouses. These parts then went duty free to factories on the Mexican side to be assembled into a final product only to be returned to the U.S. warehouse for shipment elsewhere in the world. This system came to be known as 'Mequiladora' from the Spanish "maquillar" meaning "to assemble". It is a word play for the process of parts assembly.

The effect was only slightly less than miraculous. In 1983, exports from the maquiladora zone represented 12percent of total Mexican exports; by 1994 this figure had risen to 58percent. The bad news for workers— wages in the zone were 50percent of those outside the zone in Mexico.[6] In less than six years the number of workers employed doubled from a little more than 550,000 to over a million. The population from 1983 to the present has also grown astronomically. This zone has blossomed since the creation of NAFTA in 1994.

---

[6] ILO, Labour market effects under CUFTA/NAFTA, 1999 as quoted in http://local.attac.org/13/documents/ZF_en.PDF

Where did the workers come from? The border regions were essentially unpopulated in 1965 except for a few dense cities. The throng of workers came from agricultural regions all over México where wages were sporadic and low. The people came thinking there were lots of jobs and that the pay would be good. For some any job was better than no job. Once arriving, they discovered what economic migrants discover in every age, there were too few jobs for all the people.

The throng also came ill prepared to a place even less prepared for them. As in most migrations, young and able men came and some also brought wives or girl friends. Entrepreneurs, always ready for the quick buck, saw opportunity and began bus service from isolated areas advertising the rumor that jobs were plentiful and the end of the rainbow rested on the northern border. The young people arrived without work, without much experience in finding a job, without housing, without much money, and without a social net of services to aid them.

México had in many respects created itself a huge infrastructural problem. The blossoming border cities had inadequate streets, water and sewer infrastructure, electricity, and little housing to speak of. So the people made do by building houses out of discarded cardboard, tin, corrugated steel and aluminum, and plywood. Some found abandoned school buses and moved in. Sanitation facilities were little more than latrines next to each house. Trash blew in the winds. Pollution bathed the soil. Health problems escalated. The government was slow and often incapable of responding to the need. In effect, the government had created a monster.

For the men there was more bad news. The factories needed persons with fine motor skills and manual dexterity. So the young women who came often found work before the men they came with. The machismo of the males was crushed and alcohol and drug abuse skyrocketed.

The women became pregnant. Separated by thousands of kilometers from their family, there were no services to counsel them, provide pre-natal care, or emotional and spiritual support. The social problems were mammoth and so were the spiritual needs. The women and men needed the support community of home, but on the border, no such community existed.

Presbyterian Border Ministry was founded because the National Presbyterian Church of México (INPM) could see the transformation that began in 1965 and was continuing and many U.S. Presbyterians saw needs and responded with compassion. The INPM had a vision to create a plan and came to the Presbyterian Churches of the U.S. to ask to create a binational ministry that would establish churches and provide for the social needs of the people. Yet, INPM had a larger vision. This time around the mission would be binational and mutual. There was to be no stronger and weaker, no dominant and subservient. All decisions were to be done through the work of binational committees and, as far as was possible, the mission would be carried out as equal partners sharing their gifts.

This book is a celebration of the nearly thirty years of ministry, a ministry that has:
- modeled mutual mission,

- learned in practice how to be true partners in ministry and mission,
- succeeded in establishing churches,
- provided a host of social ministries,
- educated the churches of both countries about mission and the affect our lives in the U.S. have on the peoples of other nations,
- provided innumerable churches an opportunity for serving in a mission context,
- nurtured young people in mission service,
- learned more fully what mutual mission is,
- and, with God's inspiration, grown spiritually.

Thirty years is not a long time but it is long enough for the visionaries, the founders, the many volunteers and mission workers from México and the U.S. to grow old, their memories fade, and in some cases die. Since people do not write long and descriptive letters these days; minutes of meetings are more and more sparse with little of the meeting conversations recorded; and archives are less and less complete; the personal memories and testimonies of folk are what we have. So what follows is the result of long hours of interviews, transcription, and additional research.

Having grown over the years to know many of the people I interviewed, I know none will want to be given honor for their work. All honor and glory are the Lord's. However, the Lord appreciates, and we can too, the incredible commitment, energy, imagination, and love of the people who have served and are serving as mission workers or volunteers, whether Mexican or North American, as our brothers and sisters in Mexico refer to those form the U.S. This book is an honor to write because it tells the story of an incredible miracle of God.

The title was chosen for two reasons: 1. "La frontera" is Spanish for "the border" and is a literal translation, with "frontier" being the English cognate for the Spanish word. 2. "Frontier" has multiple meanings meanings. It refers both to the border, to a new place with unknown possibilities and dangers, and to the major shift in mission focus that laid the future of mission on the line, so to speak. The spirit had led the Mexican and U.S. Presbyterians, as you shall see, to a new and parallel understanding of mission work that sought to overcome the paternalistic, colonialist style of doing mission. Not an easy task and one that has suffered a major set back to the relationship between the INPM and the PCUSA. Officially, the two national churches were on board with the plan, but the grass roots in both churches were not invested in it. This book attempts to tell the story.

There are three parts. The first will deal with the vision for the ministry that arose within the Mexican church and in a parallel fashion in the churches of the U.S. The binational nature of the plan was a result of the history of the relationship between the Mexican and U.S. churches which has its roots perhaps in the growing independence of México from U.S. economic and political domination.[7]

The second part will describe the ministries and their histories which encompasses the binational ministry of Presbyterian Border Ministry and the six locations where the work is focused. I will trace the development of these ministries through the stories of the former and present coordinators and participants. I hope to fully represent the stories of both Mexican and U.S. experiences. A part of the story is the challenges, but the challenges have led to victories and miracles. I use miracle in the sense of the incredible unintended and unforeseen consequences of the work and ministry of the servants of God.

The final part is about the future. PBM is a living experience. If the national churches had pooled their resources and learned more deeply from the experiences of twenty-seven years, I fully believe PBM would have continued to grow and flourish because of the creative prophetic imaginations of those who serve along the border and those who attend the now numerous churches. Were the founders all able to testify, I imagine none would have imagined that in thirty years the ministry would have grown so incredibly as to shift the center of gravity of the National Presbyterian Church

---

[7] Some may recoil at the reference to U.S. political domination. However, México has experienced several wars or U.S. invasions in the last couple of centuries that resulted in its loosing nearly half its historical lands, and many lives. During the Mexican Revolution (1914 to 1917), the U.S. sent an expeditionary force into México to try and capture General Poncho Villa. Mexicans recognize that the U.S. has come to its aid several times economically, most recently during the debt crisis of the 1980s, but that assistance came with draconian stipulations.

northward. As will be narrated, the decision of the INPM to severe relationships with the PCUSA has changed the nature of the work but not brought it to an end.

So the question is, Where does the ministry go from here? In the final part I hope to draw together the imaginations of those who are a part of the ministry to suggest a prospectus. I only pray that I do justice to this fertile vision.

Part I: A Vision for Binational Ministry[8]

Chapter 1:
Disengagement toward Cooperation

In the introduction, I mentioned the two conferences of U.S. and European churches that made decisions regarding the work of Christ's church in the world without giving even feigned interest in how the members of that church in the developing world might think about those decisions. Those two meetings—one in Cincinnati, Ohio in 1914 and the other in Panama City, Panama in 1916— represent the *modes operandi* of international mission work until the later part of the

---

[8] The following is heavily dependent on the work of Jerry Stacy in his history, the document in Appendix B "Presbyterian Border Ministry: Program History, Goals and Organization", and on interviews with many persons. I will not cite specific sources unless it seems prudent to do so. For the extensive history please refer to Jerry Stacy's work.

20th century. That is to say, the U.S. and European churches imposed their understanding of mission work on the indigenous churches of the nations where we were doing missions. The indigenous church had little to no say.

That approach resulted in:

1. **No truly indigenous church developing.** Because the focus was not on raising up leadership to take over the reins of leadership, the indigenous churches did not develop as such. In fact, the indigenous churches sang the hymns of European and U.S. Christians translated to their language. Instead of having music that suited the culture of the indigenous church, the music was that of the mother church. While most mission workers sought to learn the languages of their host country, in many where English, French, Spanish or Portuguese had become the official language through colonialism, services and business was done in the colonial not the indigenous language. No need was felt for translation of the Bible and hymns into native languages.

As time passed, understanding developed and wiser mission workers began to understand that if the gospel was going to be heard and responded to, Bibles need to be translated into the language of the people which led to the creation of Bible societies for that purpose. However, when hymns were translated, they retained the music of the first world churches.

The mission workers also tended to teach their cultural norms as if those norms were Christian norms. Most obvious was that they taught appropriate dress was European or U.S. dress and must replace native dress.

The legacy of that colonialist attitude remains today in African nations where men and women will dress in native costume in the villages where they live but change to colonial dress when entering the towns or cities where colonialism is still a dominant culture.

Instead of seeking to understand the gospel in the context of the indigenous people, the mission workers imposed the theology and practices of the Euro-U.S. churches on cultures that only vaguely comprehended most of the theology and, in many cases, the practices. The result was that the indigenous people of the mission field who converted tended to do so when they were most amenable to westernization or because of a material need the mission station met.

2. **A long lasting paternalism of mother church to child church.** Failure to develop leadership of indigenous people and the lingering belief that black, brown, yellow, and red skinned people were unable to be in charge left the mission workers in decision making roles. With few exceptions missionary schools and seminaries were staffed by Euro-U.S. personnel or indigenous persons closely supervised by mission personnel.

Despite many young leaders with incredible skill and biblical and theological acumen, the mission workers tended not to believe the indigenous church was capable of independence, so like a parent that would not let go, the Euro-U.S. churches always had reasons why their sons and daughters could not cut the umbilical cord.

In México, that attitude met with "youthful rebellion" in 1919 when the Presbyterian Church in México rejected the Cincinnati plan. However, their dependence on the U.S. for leadership and funding for growth meant they could do little but protest. In the late 1960s that "youthful rebellion" grew up and the National Presbyterian Church of México (INPM) requested that the Presbyterian Churches of the U.S., with the exception of the Reformed Church of America, withdraw all mission workers from México by 1972.[9]

The Rev. R. Saúl Tijerina, a leader and several times moderator of the INPM, saw the decision as a positive move towards full maturity. Others in the INPM saw the action as one more step in overcoming colonialism quoting Benito Juárez, president of México for various terms from 1858 to 1872), "Poor México, so far from God and so close to the United States." México was never officially a colony of the U.S., but the U.S. often behaved as if it were. The feeling that the northern neighbor sought many ways to dominate México runs deep and the people of the INPM felt it as deeply as anyone.

That does not mean none of the Presbyterians in México lacked appreciation for the Presbyterian Churches in the U.S. Even today one hears Mexican Presbyterians refer to the U.S. Presbyterians as the mother of the INPM. Yet, children must always grow up and develop their own independence. The Rev. Dr. Tijerina and others in the INPM hoped that a time of moratorium would provide space for the INPM to mature and break their habits of the paternalistic/colonialist model and be able in the future to once again work together in a new model.

---

[9] The Reformed Church of America was working in Chiapas at the time.

Chapter 2:
The U.S./México Border Late 1970s

By the end of the decade of the 1970s, much was changing in México as a result of the creation of the Free Trade Zone along the border.[10] The once sleepy towns and cities on the México side of the border soon became growing industrial cities teeming with persons working in newly created jobs and others seeking jobs in the new factories and businesses. The influx of people seeking work far exceeded preparations for their arrival. The industriousness and inventiveness of the Mexican people helped alleviate much of the pending crisis. Despite lack of housing and infrastructure, the migrants from other parts of México found ways to meet their basic needs although the solutions were inadequate in the end. Within a few years communities tripled in

---

[10] See above page 8.

population and were likely to do so again in a few more years. Local officials and resources were overwhelmed.

With people come typical human needs. Roads, water, septic systems, electrical grids, housing, clothing, health, education, recreation, and so on were nowhere to be found. Everywhere one turned, people were opening businesses to meet the demands, but nothing could make up for the lack of financial resources among the overwhelming majority of new residents. Pay in the factories was notoriously less than the same work would demand elsewhere in México. Despite ten hour days and six day weeks, the pay was abominably low so most households needed three or four persons working to meet the family needs.

Churches on the U.S. side of the border became concerned for their neighbors to the south and began outreach ministries to build housing, provide clothing closets, and food banks to somehow assure that nutrition and shelter would be available. One might say that Presbyterian Border Ministry began with such work, and that is in part true.

Our Presbyterian brothers and sisters to the south also saw the need and wanted to respond. They had a problem—due to the Cincinnati Plan there were no Presbyterians to speak of in the north of México with the exception of the few in Monterrey. The INPM had long wanted to start new churches in the north of the country, but lacked the resources. The INPM plan lacked church planting capacity. It seemed a good idea for each local church to be responsible for starting new churches, but like churches everywhere each church struggles to maintain itself let alone start new ones. Without

Presbytery or other help from outside, church planting suffered   with the exception of the Baja peninsula, where Baja Presbyterian Missions, a mission organization of Presbyterians in southern California, was at work. The purpose of BPM was to fund the development of new churches in México in the states of Baja California and Baja California del Sur.[11]

Now the INPM had two problems in the north. They had hundreds of Presbyterians who had left traditional Presbyterian regions and moved to the border, persons ready and able to do ministry where they lived but lacking resources as most were poor. Also, there was a growing social need that any Christian would wish to respond to. The Rev. Dr. Tijerina and others in México had a vision. At the same time in the U.S., the Presbyterian Church U.S. and the United Presbyterian Church U.S.A. were developing a coordinated study of migration issues with a concern for the U.S./México border.

---

[11] Interview with Robert Battenfield, May, 2013.

Chapter 3:
Developing Idea Binational Mutual Mission[12]

The desire of the INPM never was to completely break off relationships with the Presbyterian Churches of the U.S. but to claim independence and not enter into new dependent relationships. The Rev. Dr. Tijerina was aware of the increasingly difficult situation in the border regions and saw the present circumstances as an opportunity to move his church to a new relationship for future cooperation between it and the U.S. Presbyterian Churches. In 1971, the INPM had drafted and adopted a document titled: "A New Relation in Mission" which developed the vision and the proposal to permit re-engagement with the U.S. churches without the paternalistic/colonialist past.

---

[12] This section is heavily dependent on the testimonies of Jerry Stacy and his short book and Hector and Genie Zavaleta who provided me detailed information from Hector's well kept notes on the work.

For several years the United Presbyterian Church and the Presbyterian Church U.S. had been holding conversations with a hope for re-uniting after a lengthy division that occurred when the southern states seceded from the Union forming the Confederate States of America. The two denominations began to meet for their annual General Assemblies in the same city holding joint worship and social gatherings while doing their ecclesiastical business separately. That gave opportunity to the INPM and to the U.S. churches.

In 1979 the two denominations met in Kansas City where they received a letter from the INPM introducing "A New Relation in Joint Mission".[13] The letter says:

My Dear Brothers in Christ:

I always give thanks to God for all of you and for the Grace of God that has been given to you in Jesus Christ. I. Cor. 1:4.

The General Assembly of the Presbyterian Church of México, in its regular meeting of July 12-18, 1978, considered its relationship with the cooperating churches of the United States of North America

---

[13] See Appendix A and also "Proposal: Joint Resolution for UPCUSA/PCUS General Assemblies (México)"; Minutes of the 119th General Assembly, Presbyterian Church US Part I, Journal, Kansas City, Missouri, May 22-30, 1979, p.194. This same year the PCUS received and included action on overtures from Tres Rios and Del Salvador Presbyteries for a task force with the UPCUSA to study the many issues and concerns regarding Mexican Migration and U.S. policy toward México. The study was to include recommendations for Mission policy.

It was agreed that we maintain an official relationship with those operating churches that participated in the provision of the document "A New Relation in Mission", of 1971; and also a special commission has been set up to develop the guidelines for our relations.

We thank the Lord for the help our church has received since its foundation. We would like very much to exchange future thoughts with you about our future relationship.

"The Light in the Shadow Shines" John 1:5[14]

Presbyter Juan Garcia Martinez, Sr.

In "A New Relation in Mission", the INPM demonstrated that it was indeed a mature church capable of thinking clearly about theology and the way Christians can best do mission. The proposal included a clear statement of the theological principles that should guide the future mission relationships between INPM and the Presbyterian churches of the U.S. or other nations. The document begins with a statement of the INPM's Reformed theology which is a bow to the older churches to the north which taught them that theology. Then it concludes:

We believe that the National Presbyterian Church of México has reached her maturity and autonomy and we

---

[14] This is a clumsy translation recorded in the minutes and quoted here. A better translation is "The light shines in the darkness."

acknowledge its Constitution, Discipline, Liturgy, and Order of Worship as the norms that govern its organization and life. Therefore, we declare these THEOLOGICAL PRINCIPLES to be the determining basis of faith, of the work and of the relationships that the National Presbyterian Church of México establishes with other ecclesiastical bodies and missionary entities.

The principles that follow the theological statement seem so apparent today that we may fail to see their profound nature in 1979 when paternalism was still a strong element in mission relationships. The two main principles are autonomy and interdependence. I quote them at length because my summaries may not be adequate.

1. Autonomy. We acknowledge that the Holy Spirit, in his sovereignty, has incorporated into the Church those of us who evidence a wide variety of ministries, abilities and methods of work in the spread of the Gospel. From this it is inferred that it is He who has also bestowed on us a self-identity that demands mutual respect, understanding and complementation in the tasks He has entrusted to us. Therefore, we respect other churches and missionary entities and, by the same token, we ask for respect of the particular expression of our understanding of Biblical doctrine and the execution of our task as well as the culture and idiosyncrasy of our Country.

2. Interdependence. It is evident that the task of

evangelization of our own country and the whole world cannot be undertaken either by isolated efforts or by exclusive ministries. The need is imposed on every one of us to enter into a spirit of true interdependence that will make wise use of our particular gifts and the resources within our reach. We cannot ignore that there are at least three ways in which this interdependence is to be practiced that is:

(1) IN PARALLEL FORM, when two entities recognize their own identity and they work in a parallel form, joining efforts occasionally in short term projects and tasks.

(2) IN MUTUAL RESPECT, when two entities acknowledge the presence of each other and they establish relations of reciprocity and interchange, but in complete respect of the personality, the territorial rights and the methods of work of each other, having joint labors in just a few occasions.

(3) IN COMPLETE FUSION, where such identification of purposes, efforts, objectives and ideals is reached that there exist no distinctions between a church as such and a missionary entity of a different origin from the other. As the National Presbyterian Church of México we believe that the biblical imperative calls us

> to establish relations by the Holy Spirit,
> with no loss of our identity and inherent
> rights.

The section concludes with

> We wish above all to express a mutual
> submission to the lordship of Christ, as head
> of the Church, and to our Heavenly Father as
> the One who issued the eternal plan of
> salvation of men and to the Holy Spirit as
> infallible Guide of the Church according to the
> clear guidelines of his Holy Word.15

The U.S. churches responded to the letter with an action affirming the growth and maturity of the INPM and proposing a response that paralleled the themes stated in the "A New Relation in Mission".

U.S. Presbyterians were already concerned about the border regions. As a member of the National Council of Churches, the Presbyterians were involved in Migrant Ministries, a program that raised the level of awareness along the border. The result was studies into the plight of migrants and how the church could respond specifically at the border. One result was the founding of Proyecto Verdad in El Paso/Ciudad Juárez in 1973. This ministry was eventually followed with the establishment of Puentes de Cristo (PdC) in McAllen/Reynosa in 1980. When PdC was founded, the U.S. Presbyterians were engaged in studying their response to the issue as ordered by the General Assemblies in 1979 in response

---

15 I recognize the gender specific language of the document but seek only to maintain the historical document.

to overtures from Tres Rios and Del Salvador Presbyteries with support from the Migrant Ministries of the various presbyteries and synods.

"The Joint Task Force on Migration Issues In México-U.S. Relations" was charged

> to prepare a report on the background and present factors related to the current and projected migration of large numbers of Mexican Nationals to the United States, in the context of the overall relations between the United States and México, including recommendations for Mission policy and direction for the Presbyterian Church in the United States, in the areas of public policy, advocacy, service and ministry.[16]

The task force was appointed including Presbyter Samuel Trinidad and Elder Rafael Huicochea both from Toluca, State of México near México City. There were a number of members who were Mexican by heritage with strong connections with the INPM. The report was received in 1981 by the two U.S. General Assemblies meeting in Houston, Texas at which time the "Joint Commission on Mission" (JCM) was created and tasked as a Binational commission to develop joint mission work between the U.S. and Mexican Presbyterian Churches.

In addition to the work begun by the Task Force on Migration, the mission agencies of the two U.S. churches were re-writing their policy statements and turning the

---

[16] PCUSA Minutes, p. 104.

mission ship from paternalistic colonialism towards partnership.[17] The language of mutuality and partnership became the predominate theme of the policy and would become the preferred language in the future. The problem is not the recipe but the dish. Developing truly mutual partnerships is easier said than done. Even today as we partake of the fruits of this recipe, we find lumps in the pudding.

Under the direction of the JCM, Juan Leandro Garza, de Cristo Presbytery in Arizona, began researching possible locations for the border ministries in Arizona. In early 1984, Dr. Tijerina, Dr. Jack Bennett of the PCUS Mission Agency, and Hector Zavaleta representing the UPC, joined Leandro to visit the border regions. They returned a recommendation for locating the first site at Douglas, AZ/Agua Prieta, Sonora. (See next section for more details on the decision.)

Although the INPM had been thinking in terms of new mission relationships with U.S. Presbyterians, obtaining approval for the Border Ministry was not easy. The INPM was largely located in the southern part of México, with one lonely community of Presbyterians in Monterrey, it was not focused on nor did it clearly understand the possibilities to the north. The Rev. Dr. Tijerina, whose life and ministry had been in the north in Monterrey, was aware and energetic in his advocacy for work on the northern border but lacked sufficient

---

[17] The full reporting of the GA actions of the PCUS and UPCUSA are beyond the bounds of this work, however, the minutes of both churches report on these parallel actions. The PCUS minutes for 1980 pp. 234-241 address these themes, especially p. 239 under section d.4 "Partnerships".

support from his southern Presbyterian brothers and sisters.

He worked with sensitivity to his church's history and sought to engage the U.S. churches to pursue the work. With the help of the Joint Task Force on Migration of the U.S. churches and the JCM support was garnered from the two U.S. churches for a cooperative ministry on the border. With that support, he went to the General Assembly of the INPM with representatives of the JCM to seek support for the new mission venture in northern México. Those representatives included: Rafael Aragon, executive for Hispanic ministries in Southern California; Roberto Delgado, staff of the Synod of Texas; Hector Zavaleta, executive for Hispanic Ministries in Synod of Arizona; and Lupe Sanchez, Director of Arizona Farm Workers. The plan had been well developed and met the concerns that the Mexicans made clear in their "New Mission Relations" resolution, so being satisfied with the proposal for Border Ministry, the INPM approved a resolution opening a new period of relations between themselves and "cooperating churches and missionary entities" for the purpose of "New Fields". The first of those fields included the border states of México and those just south of the border states. The second included the central states, all of which also lacked much Presbyterian presence.

Part of their proposal was to cooperate with partners in work in the partner country to work among Spanish speaking people and to participate in activities that would contribute to "enriching fraternal relationships". Personnel would not be under the sole jurisdiction of the sending church but would be examined by the receiving church for purity of doctrine. Clearly, educational opportunities would be provided to develop indigenous leadership in the INPM for the purpose of decreasing the participation of the "cooperating churches," meaning in this case the sister churches in the U.S., a recognition that for many years the goal of U.S. Presbyterian mission had never been to develop the leadership personnel of the INPM.

A careful reading of "A New Relation in Mission" demonstrates the care with which the INPM invites the U.S. churches into relationship but fences that relationship so that it will be mutual and binational and not paternalistic. The requirement that all personnel sent to work in México by the U.S. churches would be examined by the INPM and work under its authority assured its autonomy. Prior to the moratorium the INPM had no authority over the U.S. personnel nor did it have a say in who the personnel would be. With the creation of the new relationship, that changed radically.

Chapter 4: The Development of the Plan and Its Missiological Approach[18]

When it came time to begin developing the work, the JCM did not have to start from scratch. Jack Bennet was successful in acquiring funding for the work to begin from the Mission Agency of the PCUS, and, as suggested above, Presbyterians were engaged in mission work along the border, however, the work was being carried out by U.S. Presbyterians who saw a need, had a vision and were deploying their resources. They had no Presbyterians to partner with on the other side of the border. At least, most of them did not know there were any.

In places like El Paso, the Presbyterian Churches were not aware of the moratorium on mission workers from the U.S. They saw the factories across the border,

---

[18] Once more I am dependent on interviews with the Jerry Stacy and the Zavaletas, but also with Bob Battenfield who has been associated for many years with Baja Presbyterian Mission and Pueblos Hermanos.

the growing population and the plight of the people and an opportunity manifested itself in their souls. They responded by organizing around the idea of providing a ministry to meet social needs and starting a Presbyterian Church that would be a socially conscious church. They contacted the General Assembly and asked for guidance. They learned of the Rev. Dr. Tijerina and approached him. His response was one of vision. Because he knew his church lacked resources to deploy to the border, he wanted to assist this effort that he hoped would spread along the border, he gave counsel and advice when asked.

Under the work of Proyecto Verdad a new church was formed and ministries were developed to meet the medical, dental, and other social needs of the people. The vision was that the church would be a *serviglesia* or a servant church, meaning a church that would see themselves as doing more than preaching the gospel but living out the mandate of Matthew 25:31-46. Despite the moratorium, Dr. Tijerina and other Mexicans met with the board of Proyecto Verdad.

Seeing the growing human need, the leadership of the project was impatient for the complete development of churches and began to develop the social ministries in various locations. By the time of the formation of the JCM, Proyecto Verdad had helped establish Puentes de Cristo in 1981 which funded the construction of a church building, community center, and staff salaries.

Predating these two projects by a decade was Baja Presbyterian Missions (BPM) in the San Diego area. BPM had as its primary goal the construction of churches and assistance in staffing them. Operating as a nonprofit religious organization to raise and allocate resources, BPM did not desire to place personnel from the U.S. in México but to enable the INPM to place personnel in the Baja to proclaim the gospel, thus it was in harmony with the INPM in two ways: 1. BPM was not sending personnel and 2. it sought to fulfill a primary desire of the INPM, namely, to start new churches in the "new fields".

All this meant that when the JCM formed the Binational Border Committee, soon to be known as the Joint Mission Commission (JMC), under the leadership of the Mexican Coordinator The Rev. Dr. Tijerina and the U.S. Coordinator the Rev. Jerry Stacy, the ground had been plowed and the fields planted in three regions. Two already trained mission couples—Rev. William and Mrs. Susan Soldwisch and Rev. Gary and Mrs. Beth Waller—were assigned to the border region before the actual site locations were determined.

The decision to make Agua Prieta/Douglas the first official PBM site resulted from consideration of places within the Synod that led to the conclusion that AP/Douglas was the best place. As Hector Zavaleta explained, "We looked at Nogales and Naco and Agua Prieta. We believed that two conditions were important. One was that the scale of the work was doable and the second was that there be an active Presbyterian Church close enough to cooperate in the work. There was no church closer to Nogales than Valley Presbyterian Church in Green Valley and they seemed uninterested. The closest church to Naco was in Bisbee and it was small and not very active. In Douglas there was a church that at one time had been a merged congregation of Anglo and Hispanic Presbyterians. The pastor and session were interested in the work and even wrote us a letter to that effect. So we decided on AP/Douglas." (Interview, July, 2013). Despite beginning in AP/Douglas, the ministry plan at first included the idea that the co-coordinators would also have responsibilities for Naco and Nogales.

Presbyterian Border Ministry (PBM) is filled with amazing providential stories. Shirley Jewell tells how the Wallers and others were just beginning to work on a plan to get started when one afternoon a knock came to the door of the Waller home in Douglas. Remember people could still freely walk between Douglas and Agua Prieta. Beth Waller answered the door with dish and dish towel in hand. A Mexican woman was standing outside and they exchanged pleasantries when the Mexican woman explained that she had heard there were Presbyterians trying to start a church in Agua Prieta and that she was a Presbyterian. The dish dropped and broke on the steps. After exchanging apologies, they got back to business and Sister Amelia del Pozo, known to all as Hermana Amelia, became a founding member and matriarch of the Lily of the Valleys Church in Agua Prieta and what became Frontera de Cristo was born. For the next year or so, Bible studies and worship services were held in her home in Agua Prieta.

On December 10, 1984 the first meeting of the Provisional Local Committee on AP/Douglas met with the following attendees: Manny Valenzuela, Shirley Jewell, George Frazier, Wayne Leipold, Arlo Janssen,

Don Gray, Beth and Gary Waller (appointed by both PCUSA and the National Presbyterian Church of México), and Bob Seel (member of the Joint Commission on Mission and Presbytery Executive of de Cristo Presbytery). By March 17, 1985 Luis Manuel Lugo had arrived to begin work as the INPM Coordinator for the work in Agua Prieta/Douglas. The May 7 minutes reported that the first meeting of the Presbyterian Church in Agua Prieta was to take place May 12 in the home of Amelia del Pozo. The committee had chosen to submit the name of "Frontera de Cristo" for approval as the ministry name. Mission groups began coming to learn about the ministry and contributions for the work began to flow in enabling the work to proceed rapidly.

The commission then decided to join the existing work in southern California and the Baja begun by Baja Presbyterian Missions and in 1984 the Soldwisches went to San Diego to work with the Presbytery of San Diego and the Mexican leadership to form Pueblos Hermanos. The Coordinators Stacy and Tijerina worked with the already existing ministries of Proyecto Verdad and Puentes de Cristo to fold them into the overall plan. That work seemed to bear fruit, but five years later, Proyecto Verdad collapsed due to the failures of the Co-coordinators to accept the vision and their incapacity to work collegially with the Mexican partners who decided to leave the work. The Mexican partners requested a severance with Proyecto Verdad demonstrating the difficulty of the vision and its work.[19]

These ministries and activities were being guided by persons who had a peculiar, for the time, vision of doing mission work. In fact, the vision of a binational mutual mission had not been practiced anywhere. Even thirty years after PBM began, the vision is not widely shared or understood. When I used the terms with a Roman Catholic priest and friend, he was surprised by it and a bit confused. He asked a few questions about what the vision was and then said, "That is so far from the way Roman Catholics work, it boggles the mind." When PBM was getting up and running, its vision for doing mission boggled the minds of Presbyterians in both countries not because they couldn't understand the idea, but because our habits were so ingrained it was difficult to actually make sense of it. Thirty years after doing this work and seeking to practice mission this way with the INPM and other national churches around the world, the majority of U.S. Presbyterians continue to think missions is about going, doing and giving and do not expect to receive anything from those whom they serve.

To reiterate, the vision can be easily stated but not so easily practiced. The vision essentially:

1. created a mission partnership between the INPM and the PCUSA.
2. stated that partnership would be shaped by:
   • recognition of mutual autonomy,

---

[19]Document in archives of the Presbyterian Border Ministry "1989 Crisis at Puentes and Verdad". Also, interviews of several of those mentioned in footnote 18 and including, the Rev. Bob Seel.

- sharing of the unique gifts given by God to the two partners,
- a sense of interdependence of the people of God in the mission of Christ.

Up to this point, the work of the church had not been thought of in general as a partnership and full partnership of a daughter church with its mother church was a difficult change in the dynamic. It is as hard for children to claim their autonomy as it is for the parent to recognize and live through it. As the project began to develop, these same strains developed.

Proyecto Verdad, one of the oldest cross border ministries, came to an end in 1989 because the U.S. members of the board and the U.S. co-coordinator had one vision while the Mexican co-coordinator and board members had another vision. Ultimately, the Mexican partners believed they had to accept the U.S. vision or get out, so they asked that the partnership be dissolved.[20] It took ten years before the wounds had healed sufficiently to reinitiate a ministry in Ciudad Juárez and El Paso.

---

[20] see note 19.

Part II: 1984—Initiating the Plan

Chapter 1: The Border Conditions

When the staffing of the Binational Border Committee was formed, the border was in process of continuing transformation. Most of the towns and cities along the Mexican side had seen and were seeing new factories set up. The influx of people from the south was overwhelming the communities. Sleepy towns such as Agua Prieta were becoming cities and places like Ciudad Juárez, Nogales, Tijuana, Nuevo Laredo, and Reynosa grew beyond the capacity of either the national, state and municipal government's capacity to meet the infrastructural needs. In fact, the government was having difficulty meeting the needs of the corporations locating in the border regions, a priority for creating jobs and growing the economy.

In many of the cities, street plans had been created and lots surveyed, so people were not settling willy nilly. For the new residents, transportation to work was a problem because few had cars or bicycles. The larger factories developed their own bus system and continue to maintain them. Some of the larger cities had bus systems, but with the population explosion, the systems were inadequate.

In many cases the new, largely poor residents were looked down on by the older more settled residents. The new areas were for the most part shabby huts of whatever kind of material that could be salvaged. Bathrooms were often just a latrine resulting in odors and, when it rained, sanitation concerns. Crime seemed to skyrocket and the new residents were largely blamed and animosity developed.

Poverty was not new to the border towns and cities, but it was not worse than other parts of México until the influx of people began. Then the border became known for a teeming population of the poor. Even those who were lucky enough to get jobs, remained in poverty unless at least three persons in a family were able to work. Then the family would have resources to begin improving their lot.

People without work found ways to live or they descended into despair. A few ways to make a living on the border were to get involved with the drug trade for the young men and prostitution for the young girls. The border towns had been known for these two activities for years servicing U.S. military and civilian populations and, as time passed, the drug trade and prostitution increased.

Because of the poverty and resulting social issues, the various ministries instituted programs to meet social needs such as medical and dental clinics and fairs, clothing closets, food pantries, infant supplies; classes on self-esteem, nutrition and infant care and the like. The church planting activities began as soon as Mexican and U.S. pastoral personnel could be found and placed. U.S. Presbyterian Churches in the region, moved by compassion for the poor, responded to the new ministries with donations of material resources and financial support.

The one thing that had not changed yet was border enforcement. One could just walk across the border almost everywhere just as Sister Amelia had when she wanted to meet the Presbyterians who had come to start a church. (See out take above). There was a U.S. Border Patrol presence in densely populated areas, but it was minimal. The purpose at the time did not focus on searching and finding undocumented people but dealt with suspicious activity. Driving across the border into the U.S. usually meant going through an official port of entry, and documents were seldom necessary because agents were primarily looking for smugglers. Going into México seldom meant stopping for anything at all unless one was in a van or truck. Then the Mexican authorities would check to see if one was bringing cargoes that were prohibited. The casualness of the border made coming and going for both the U.S. and the Mexican participants in the binational committees fairly simple. The committees could meet on either side or alternate sides and be sure that members could show up.

Chapter 2: Difficulties

Challenges arise in every human endeavor. It was not long before the challenges for PBM began. Needless to say, creating a new ministry that spans a border 2,000 miles long with the largest disparity of economic wealth to poverty anywhere in the world is challenge enough. The practical concerns were legion.

Property

Since the revolution of 1914, churches in México were not allowed to own property so the church had to petition the government for property. That usually meant finding available land, not a particularly difficult thing to do, but then to communicate with the owner about whether he was willing to sell. The owners often did not want to sell to a church for reasons of prejudice or because working with the government was difficult when a church was involved. Sometimes the ministries were able to find land still owned by the government, however, things did not go easily. There were documents, letters, assurances, and bribes to be paid. Being church programs, there was a general rule against paying bribes which meant much longer wait times.

Once the property was acquired, a building had to be built. Fairly soon after initiating the projects work delegations began to come to do such things. Dependence on volunteers from the U.S. meant the construction was slow and often quality was lacking, but a building of low quality was better than none. Until a building was built the churches met in the homes of those who became members or adherents.

Once the building was built, it needed electricity. Once more that meant interacting with the government, making petitions, writing letters and so on. One church group began meeting in their building and used candles in the evening meetings for light before they could get electricity. When one of the leaders heard that there was a rumor that Presbyterians were witches, the leader said something had to be done so they worked out with a neighbor to "borrow" his electricity.

Cultural Differences

Practical issues, as daunting as they may seem, are seldom the greatest of difficulties. Nearly every person I interviewed talked about the cultural differences between Mexicans and Americans. The Rev. Jésus Gallegos said:

> Mexicans have an idea, get excited and get to work on it. Then there is a ministry committee meeting and the idea is put on the table for

discussion. The U.S. members ask a bunch of questions. We can't answer them because we don't know, but we believe it will work. That isn't enough for the U.S. members. They want to see the goals and objectives, the plan, the steps and timeline, who will do what, and always the money. Mexicans don't think about money because they aren't accustomed to having any, so we just do it. Everything is in our heads for doing what we want, but the U.S. members want to see it on paper. When I first came to the border, I thought they were being critical of the idea or didn't think it important. It took me a long time to realize that it is just a difference of doing things. We learned to do better planning from the U.S. members. I think they learned to rely more on the Spirit. (Conversation, April, 1998)

This difficulty led to considerable conflict at several sites and a recognition that the process of discerning personnel placements had to be refined. The interview process had not taken into account differing personalities and styles of leadership, let alone theological differences which are not uniform in either country but definitely differ between the nations. Nor was training in the vision for the ministry strong so both U.S. and Mexican coordinators came with their own church's perspective without being prepared to work in a mutual and binational manner or with much experience in cross cultural relationships. "Everyone sort of knew what the other culture was like, but knowledge and experience of a culture are different. Some of us had served in other mission fields, but under a different model. How do you work in this model? We were sort of feeling our way." (Interview, Rev. Bob Seel, May 2012)

When U.S. mission delegations began to come to the border, they brought with them the U.S. culture that often conflicted with Mexican culture, especially in the church of México where Presbyterians are culturally and socially conservative. In 1984 the border churches and the pastors that came to lead them represented that conservatism: no alcohol or ·cigarettes, women wore dresses and blouses with sleeves, dancing was prohibited, showing affection in public was unacceptable. Despite efforts to train delegations about respecting the sensitivities of the Mexican Presbyterians, things happened. Teenage girls and boys brought nothing but shorts to wear, blouses without sleeves and often tank tops. At times the U.S. girls would wear midriff-showing blouses, an offense to the modesty of the hosts. When playing basketball, the U.S. boys would strip off their shirts, an absolute taboo. Adults would sneak in to corners of the property to smoke or walk down the street to light up thinking nobody would notice. Delegations would go out to eat, invite the pastor's family, and maybe some others and then buy a beer.

At first, these breaches were met with some consternation on the part of U.S. Coordinators and delegation leaders were asked to rein in their charges. Many Mexican Presbyterians wondered how deep the Christian faith of U.S. Presbyterians was. Some delegation members responded that the Mexicans were being intolerant and charged them with not being sensitive to U.S. culture. Delegation members failed to follow the rule that the guest adapts to the host's context.

Over time this issue became resolved in several ways. The Presbyterians who had come from the south of México discovered some of their dress codes were simply impractical in a region where the wind blows and whips skirts into the air. From late Spring to early Fall the heat is nearly intolerable during daylight and a little less clothing makes for a cooler body. While many parts of México from which the people come are hot and humid, they were not accustomed to the lack of shade, water, and the blistering heat of the desert son. So dress styles began to change fairly early.

The other moral issues did not change, but the Mexican Presbyterians now living on the border began to see their U.S. brothers and sisters in a different light. As the relationships developed, understanding of the other became more personal and accepting. Tolerance and cultural respect grew. That does not mean Mexican Presbyterians began to drink and smoke, but that they did not judge the U.S. Presbyterians for doing so.

Poverty

U.S. Presbyterians come from a culture accustomed to hearing the poor being blamed for being poor. In the U.S. we hear that poor people are lazy, maybe not very bright, can't handle money, lack initiative, and so on and so forth. The prejudices with regard to the poor are deeply ingrained. Oddly, many in México think likewise but those who do tend to be upper class and upper middle class. When delegations come to México, they are ill prepared for encountering poverty because they come from a country where poverty is tucked away. In México the poverty is in one's face all the time or so it seems.

The average applicant for a mission delegation will say that the reason s/he wishes to go on the trip is to help people less fortunate than they. Not a bad sentiment, but a somewhat misguided one because they usually mean the poor. However, one can be poor in different ways. The materially poor may be spiritually rich and the materially wealthy spiritually poor. Navigating this complicated distinction requires a good guide. Few U.S. Presbyterians are prepared to be such guides.

The first summer I spent at Frontera de Cristo, I had studied about the many issues facing people who were living in Agua Prieta— economy, political history, kinds of labor and factories. My family and I immersed ourselves in the life of Agua Prieta as far as our language skills permitted. We observed and shared our observations. I worked with the mission delegations which at that time were solely engaged in construction and health fairs. There was only minimal interaction with the people in the church except at worship services, despite that the delegations slept and ate primarily at the church. The delegations worked in the morning and went on recreational adventures in the U.S. in the afternoon.

What they saw of the lives of the people of Agua Prieta or the Lily of the Valleys Church was from a distance. Their hearts were touched by the poor children and families, the poor housing, the obvious malnutrition and lack of resources. So they had a heart that often broke because of what they saw, but nothing was being done then by the ministries to assist them to understand why such poverty existed or what they could do about it.

One evening my family was invited to join a delegation for dinner at a restaurant in Douglas. The delegation members were afraid to eat food in Agua Prieta because of the myths so often told about fruit and vegetables and water in México, so we were eating Mexican food at a restaurant in Douglas and one of the delegation members said, "I am glad I came here. I think it has changed my life forever." Someone asked her how her life has changed. "I'll never be able to feel sorry for myself again because I'll always remember these children."

Certainly not bad sentiments, but "always" is a very long time and such sentiments tend to fade and we all slip back into feeling sorry for ourselves, envying others, and coveting the good life as defined by Americans. I tried to think of a good way to respond to the woman and, I suppose, to the general sentiment of the group. It was difficult without sounding critical. Finally, I said, "I understand your feelings and affirm them because we all need a starting point, but maybe you can go farther." I went on to suggest they lead a study in their church on the root causes of poverty in the U.S. and the under-developed and developing countries and that they do so with the Bible to guide their understanding of how Christians should think about and respond to poverty. I also suggested they initiate a ministry that would give them the opportunity to work with the poor to deal with an issue of poverty in their home community.

When U.S. visitors find themselves immersed in abject poverty, they are often overwhelmed with its pervasiveness and the horror of its effects. Few people from the U.S. have witnessed abject poverty because our poorest people live in houses that may be substandard but few live in houses made of tar paper. Our children have several if not many changes of clothes, social services are readily available, a minimal amount of food is available to most, and if children become ill, they may receive medical treatment. In México, especially along the border, abject poverty is a constant, especially in the new communities that spring up almost overnight and nothing existed to deal with the challenges of poverty.

People from the U.S. can hardly contain their pity and want to help while their guides ask that they not help individuals but the programs that seek to provide aid. Whenever we are asked by some person to give him or her help, we struggle with that concept no matter how often we have been to the border. I was once with a delegation in a plaza where a celebration was going on and a place where beggars are constantly present at such events. People from the U.S. are easily identifiable, so a man approached several of the women in the group seeking a hand out. I saw what was happening and asked the man in Spanish to please leave us alone that we have given to organizations that provide aid. He became belligerent and I told him to leave or I would call for the police. He then became angry and I, perhaps out of anxiety for the safety of the delegation, responded a bit more forcefully that he had better leave. One of the members of the delegation asked me why I didn't just give him something. Good question.

Judgments under pressure are often difficult. Perhaps, a single dollar would have ended the moment but what of the future and of the hundreds who need that dollar. Do we give the dollar to the one most in our face or give it to support those who can make that dollar go farther still? But charity can also cause jealousy within the community. When one family finds its way into the heart of "the rich ones from the U.S." and receives contributions and favors, what does that say to the rest of the community. Certainly, we do not go to the ministry with the intent of creating divisions, but our actions often do just that especially when we understand so little the dynamics of poverty and our responses to it. (see more on this in part III).

Differing Goals

One of the biggest challenges to the beginnings of PBM and to its continuing future is the difference in goals between the two national churches and their people. As Jerry Stacy expressed it,

> The stated priority of the National Presbyterian Church of México has always been "new church" development. The U.S. focus on programs to alleviate poverty understood "new church" to mean "new servant church". Reflecting on the *serviglesia* tension, Saúl suggested that both national churches had been naive in attempting to implement the servant church model without having thought through all of the cultural and theological barriers. He said: "The National Presbyterian Church of México wrongly assumes that if a church is

established, after Bible study and prayer, its members will see the needs of the oppressed in their community and respond accordingly. The Presbyterian Church (USA), on the other hand, believes that if it establishes a clinic in a marginal community to meet health needs, the clinic will somehow, someday, by the grace of God, become a church." (Stacy, *Brief History*)

This particular divide continues to this day. I'll be discussing it in the final chapter. The differences come from a difference in primary focus. The Mexican church spent its formative years under missionaries from the U.S. for whom evangelism ranked high. Social justice and social ministry ranked quite low. One did not ignore the needs of the poor but that was not the focus of mission work in México. Since church planting and development absorbed the vision of the missionaries, the pastors and laypeople they led into Presbyterianism were led there with a theology that stressed conversion from Roman Catholicism which, as the original purposes of the vision for mission indicated, was not considered a fully Christian denomination.[21]

By the time PBM was being formed, the PCUSA churches that were first engaged in ministry on the border were responding to the great social needs of the people in México. Presbyterians in the U.S. had grown to consider faith a private matter that suppressed the

---

[21]See The 35th Annual Report (1872) of the PCUSA Board of Foreign Missions in the "Introduction". Once more this PCUSA was the historic PCUSA that predates the histories of the National PC, UPC, and PCUS.

evangelistic fervor of past ages. Despite a push in the 1950s to start new churches, the 1960s had led to little interest in new church development among U.S. Presbyterians, so that even in very fast growing regions of the country the PCUSA and its presbyteries were ·not starting new churches. The result was that the Presbyterians moving into the fast growing regions had few Presbyterian Churches from which to choose. This oversight, much overlooked in discussions of loss of membership overall in the PCUSA, resulted in a bleeding of Presbyterians to other denominations.

The INPM was focused on that very issue. Their members were going north to the border from the traditionally Presbyterian south, so the Mexican leadership recognized a need to start new churches and to spread what they perceive as the true expression of the gospel to every state in México. Thus for them new churches had to be a priority.

There was little chance that U.S. Presbyterians were going to get engaged only in starting new churches. To some extent, mission delegations and U.S. leadership bowed to the desire of the Mexicans but their focus was clearly on the social needs, building of community centers for health and dental clinics, technical education, English classes, children's programs, libraries, and, in recent years, computer labs.

That being said, the INPM did accept the community center ideas and helped fill nurse educator positions that then created a host of health advocates for the communities. Those who worked in such ministries and experienced them most intimately saw them as providing an excellent vehicle for sharing the gospel. As Marta González Rojas, Nurse for Pueblos Hermanos in Tijuana, said:

> When we began we had a trailer with a common area where they gave classes for the women, classes on self-esteem, and values to motivate the women, and we worked with the children to prevent sexual abuse, dental hygiene, arts and crafts, and I worked with the elderly. Then we began to preach the gospel. (Interview, May 2012)

PCUSA folks went to hold dental clinics and health clinics without much sense of preaching the gospel because they had grown accustomed to the idea that "they would know us by our love." Yet, the Mexicans understood that love can be shared implicitly but without explicitly saying that we are doing these things because Jesus loves you and has sent us here, the connection is probably lost.

In my summer experience I saw the two sides do their part. A mission delegation made up of a number of medical doctors and nurses came to Frontera de Cristo. They were prepared with all they needed to hold a health clinic. They even brought a Spanish language video on nutritional health. Evidently, this was all a very good idea but they had no materials for publicizing or sharing the gospel. The ministry had a TV and VCR to play the delegation's video but asked if they could also show a video that told some parables of Jesus for children and do publicity in the community. All agreed to the evangelistic idea and the event was quite successful with many diagnoses of important medical issues and many hearing the gospel perhaps for the first time. No record exists of how many if any persons became Christians or even came to the church, but another important thing happened—in an area where most people didn't know Presbyterians existed, the residents discovered that Presbyterians were good Christian people who cared for people living in poverty, and more importantly they received the explicit message that God loved them.

Differing Perspectives

The Rev. Randy Campbell, former co-coordinator of Compañeros en Misión at Nogales and presently pastor of First Presbyterian Church in Las Vegas, NM, tells of the contrast in the way people from the U.S. and México view each other. Groups had come from a wealthy church in Phoenix to do work in Nogales. They were shocked by the poverty, the number of people living in the same small houses and that all the houses seemed so small, the sanitation systems, lack of water resources, and the poor quality of the cars and trucks and the streets. Then the church invited the Mexicans to visit their church in Phoenix. Rev. Campbell said he wondered as they drove the van to Phoenix how the Mexicans would respond. They exclaimed over the shiny new cars and the beautifully landscaped yards as they traveled into Phoenix. On the return he listened with interest as one after the other remarked on some aspect of the trip. One pair lamented that the houses were colored in such a boring manner. "Why don't they paint them different colors?" one woman asked. Another observed, "It was so sad where we stayed because the sister lived all alone in a house big enough for twenty people but her children didn't want to live with her or for her to live with them." And then another, "Yes, and she had a huge car and nobody ever rode with her. Why don't they want to share anything?"

He said that none of this was said in criticism but in a sense of amazement and wonder. These are superficial observations that point to a real significant chasm in outlook and perspective and maybe faith. "But", he went on, "conversions do take place. A church from Wasilla, Alaska came to visit and they became very attached to the people in the church in Nogales and invited the people to Wasilla. The Mexicans arrived in Wasilla and the pastor from Wasilla said it was like a revival. Their visit; Their spirit; The enthusiasm with which the Mexicans shared their faith and never said anything about being poor." The whole experience simply transformed the many prejudices about México of our church members," testified the pastor.

Overcoming Arrogance and Paternalism

Old habits form slowly over the years and become entrenched, however, when it comes to cultures that have interacted for over a hundred years the habits go in both directions. Paternalism for the U.S. was so engrained as to be nearly unrecognized by church folks and when ministers, mission workers, or denominational leaders pointed it out, the criticism was responded to by anger and resentment. When making a presentation in one church, I spent some time talking about this problem in my general remarks and went on to another subject. I had noticed a woman listening very closely but becoming agitated. When I asked for questions, she was first to respond. "Who do they think they are for criticizing us when all we want to do is help?"

In fact, that is an essential question. Who do they think they are? and who do we think we are? "Many of those who were working in México before the Moratorium were humble and faithful people, but, sadly, they were overshadowed by very arrogant persons," lamented Hector Zavaleta. He went on to say that one of the things that made PBM work effectively at the PBM committee level was that the committee was made up of people on both sides of the border that understood the culture of both nations. He and Juan Leandro Garza were both Mexicans who had migrated at young ages and spent most of their lives in the U.S. but had family and memories of life in México and the Presbyterian Church in México. Saúl Tijerina, for one, had a cultural intelligence that exceeded that of almost everyone. (Interview, July 2013)

Personnel and committee members often lacked that cross cultural intelligence. Instead they had to live out Romans 12:1-2:

Therefore, I urge you, brothers and sisters, in view of God's mercy, to offer your bodies as a living sacrifice, holy and pleasing to God—this is your true and proper worship. Do not conform to the pattern of this world, but be transformed by the renewing of your mind. Then you will be able to test and approve what God's will is—his good, pleasing and perfect will. (NIV)

Not an easy task.

The U.S. Presbyterians were, it seemed, by nature paternalistic towards persons of other cultures, and often the perspective was clearly imperialistic. Despite good intentions mission personnel and delegations from churches decided what the Mexicans needed and pursued projects the Mexicans did not desire or see a need for. At one point, says Hector Zavaleta, the U.S. co-coordinator would have a delegation build a wall only to go back the next week to find the wall deconstructed. "What happened to the wall?" he'd ask. The Mexican coordinator would respond, "The church people didn't want it." The habits that caused the moratorium of the 70s were not offered readily on the altar of sacrifice.

On the Mexican side the habits of paternalism were as deeply engrained. Mexican Presbyterians had deferred to the domination of the U.S. missionaries. The habit was hard to break because the money and other material resources were coming primarily from the U.S. church because the Mexican church had barely enough money to meet requirements of their local congregations and their support for new churches. The natural thing in such circumstances is deference.

Another aspect was that when U.S. mission delegations built something, the Mexican Presbyterians sort of assumed the delegation had an ownership in the building or house. One mission worker visited a church in central México where a mission delegation had built a building with a bathroom that was not working. The missionary asked, "Why doesn't the bathroom work?" The response was, "We are waiting on the Americans to come back, so they can fix it." This attitude that sounds like dependence or laziness to the U.S. mind is an example of learned deference to the dominant party. The Mexicans did not have ownership of the building and could not fix what was not theirs. So sacrificing behaviors on the altar for the transformation of our minds cuts both ways.

Resolving Conflicts of Personnel[22]

Almost always when several organizations have some responsibility for work that needs doing, conflicts of purpose arise. For Presbyterian Border Ministry, that often was represented in personnel choices. As Jerry Stacy described it, the General Assembly World Mission's (GA) recruitment were quite good at recruiting mission workers. Once the mission workers were selected and sent to the border, PBM had the responsibility of overseeing their work with their local binational committee. When we first started, PBM assumed the vetting by World Missions would provide a person suited to the work on the border.

Not long after the beginning of the work, PBM discovered the assumption was wrong. "There was nothing pernicious", according to Stacy, "we simply did not have a good plan. GA would select a candidate that met their requirements and what they thought we needed. Sometimes we could be engaged in the interviews but most often not. When the candidates came to the border to visit, we often found deficiencies: a poor understanding of the missiological goals, differences in working styles that would conflict with the

---

[22] The following is the result of multiple interviews. Except where a specific source person is stated the information was gleaned from numerous interviews on both sides of the border.

Mexican partners, or one of those intangibles." As Hector Zavaleta pointed out, one of the U.S. mission workers had emotional problems that were not uncovered in the GA vetting process that resulted in serious problems. At times one of the mission sites would circumvent the GA process and select a person whom they knew for the job and then ask GA to appoint the person(s) as mission workers. Even that approach did not always turn out well. The results were often quite difficult to overcome. As indicated above, in one instance, Proyecto Verdad, the Mexican partners pulled out over a conflict with an U.S. Coordinator.

For Stacy and his successor, Stanley DeVoogd, the money was always a difficult issue to navigate regarding personnel. There was always a disparity between the salary of the U.S. and Mexican Coordinators which seemed unjust on the surface because they were both expected to do the same job. Yet, even with salaries below those of the U.S. coordinators, the Mexican coordinators were earning sometimes twice as much as Mexican pastors in general.

The exchange rate for the peso did not help with salary equalization. Throughout the decade of the 80s the peso devalued against the dollar precipitously. In 1983 the dollar cost 145 pesos. By 1990 a dollar cost 2,945 pesos and in 1993 3,100. At that time, México coined new pesos. The new peso exchanged for the old 3,000 to one. A dollar then cost 3.1 new pesos. As I write, the rate is 12.97 pesos to the dollar. The rate of devaluation has declined, but there have been devaluations that were disastrous such as in the Christmas devaluation of 1994 known in the Latin

World as the "December Mistake". The mistake was the decision of the newly elected president to let the value of the peso float for the first time in years. It went almost overnight to 7.1 pesos to the dollar doubling the cost of everything.

The instability of the peso, or, better put, the certainty of its continued devaluation, created an issue for PBM and its sites. When the devaluation occurs, does the ministry adjust the salaries of the Mexican coordinator so he is earning the equivalent in U.S. dollars that he did before devaluation? It is not difficult to see that doing so would produce an increasing disparity between the pastors serving as PBM coordinators and their Mexican colleagues whose salaries could not be raised by their congregations. The situation was untenable.

The issue of coordinators salaries was at least one of the issues that led to the decision to eliminate the positions of the PBM co-coordinators who oversaw the work of all the sites, reported Stanley DeVoogd. When the Rev. Tijerina retired, the INPM appointed Jorge Alvarado to be the Mexican Co-coordinator with U.S. Co-coordinator Stanley DeVoogd. Alvarado lacked the reputation and political and interpretive skills of Rev. Tijerina whose connection with all things INPM gave the sense within the INPM that it was connected to the work on the border. Rev. Tijerina was the pastor of the largest church in Monterrey from which he received a salary, so he received a small stipend and travel expenses from PBM. Rev. Alvarado, solely employed by PBM, needed a larger salary and at times asked for more while his colleagues did not think him as effective an advocate and leader of the ministry as Rev. Tijerina had been.[23] That led the PBM council to address another issue, especially important to those from México. There was never enough money to support the work of church development in México which was the primary concern of the INPM. The INPM council members began to say that the salary for the Mexican coordinator was needed for the pastors who served churches and for new pastors for new work.

Eventually, Rev. Alvarado resigned and the decision was made to eliminate that position. As time passed, Mr. DeVoogd began working to eliminate his position because he believed the six sites were sufficiently mature to be able to do their work with the support of the PBM council. Once the decision was made he resigned and the council hired a person to do administrative functions and fund raising.

From DeVoogd's point of view, the decision had a good result. Funds were immediately available for the goals of the Mexican church and both denominations became more intimately engaged with the work of PBM. That was especially true for the INPM because the Mexican ministers assumed Tijerina was taking care of things. Now the ship needed a crew and the leadership of the INPM became more engaged.

Sadly, the decision did not work as well for the future of PBM. The person hired to raise funds within the PCUSA was not well suited to the task, was not proactive in the work and lacked training in either fund raising or funds development. While all that was true,

---

[23] Interview with Stacy and others.

she did effectively carry out administrative functions on request and specific tasks assigned by the binational committee. Still, an important component of PBM was not being addressed effectively at that level, and depending on project personnel, the projects thrived or suffered.

Lacking funds for much of anything but pastoral support, and often not even having that, the INPM continued to pursue the establishment of new churches. The pastors in the presbyteries on the border worked diligently on this goal. The work never progressed suitably in the opinion of the ministers south of the border presbyteries, but neither were the pastors in the border presbyteries satisfied. Conditions on the border were simply quite different from those to the south. Between industrial work schedules and trying to establish their lives, the Presbyterians on the border found themselves unable, despite best intentions, to support the churches with time and talents much less funds.

One faithful elder with whom I became friends in the mid 1990s finally was able to bring his family to the border, buy a lot for a house and begin building it. On one visit I became aware I was not seeing his family on Sundays and asked about them. As with churches everywhere, people find themselves in conflict or disagreement and leave the church. That was not the case with my friend and his family; they only had Sundays and evenings to work on building their house. Evenings are short for the industrial worker as they usually work ten hour days, so evenings were spent gathering materials for Sunday's work. Credit was non-existent for most in México until quite recently, so whatever they needed for the house had to be bought in small amounts and no more than could be used on work days. Therefore, this family, like many others, was unable to participate in the life of the church for nearly a year. It was a big loss for the church as the father was a wise elder, counselor to the pastor and astute leader. The children, still mostly young were important participants in the youth program and the mother was a significant member of the women's fellowship.

Such a life is unimaginable to the southern Mexicans who have, for the most part, lived in stable communities in homes that only need improvements. The challenges for the southern churches lay in the exodus of so many men leaving their families and going north.

Chapter 3: Successes

NOTE: The following have accompanying slideshows and videos at: www.presbyteriansonthefrontier.net/ Books that will enrich your experience. Use username: Presbyterian and Password: Calvinandhobbes1985.

Frontera de Cristo (FdC)[24]

As stated above, FdC was the first official Border Ministry site. The General Assembly task force that was assigned to study migrant issues beginning in 1979 and reporting in 1981 included a section titled "Strangers Becoming Neighbors" which was published and sent to the churches for study. The Rev. Jerry Stacy was appointed to promote the document and lead synods, presbyteries and churches in studying and understanding it, and, hopefully, acting on it. The Synod of Arizona was ready to act and formed their own program

---

[24] Website: http://www.fronteradecristo.org.

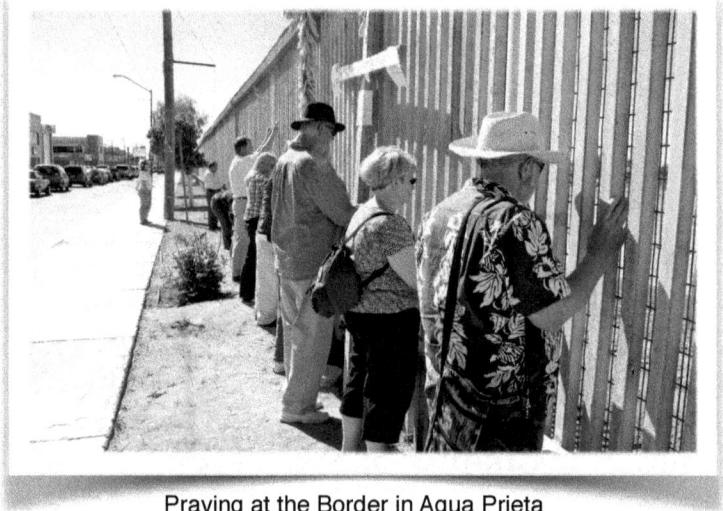

Praying at the Border in Agua Prieta

"Strangers Becoming Neighbors" leading to a proposal by Juan Leandro that a ministry be established on the synod's southern border. That led to consulting with the JCM to obtain its support which was readily given by all parties involved but, as reported above, a bit more difficult process was required to obtain support of the INPM.

At the time that decision was being made, the discovery delegation sent by the JCM stood and looked across a sandy stretch between Douglas, AZ and Agua Prieta, Sonora. There the border was marked by nothing but the monuments that still stand along the border at regular distances marking the survey by the U.S. government and accepted by México. No fence. No obstruction to crossing. As Shirley Jewel, one of the first committee members for FdC, stated, "We could just walk across wherever it was convenient. It was really like there was just one city." The porous nature of the border at the time made the work a bit easier for the co-coordinators, the board, and mission delegations than it is today.

While the JCM and the INPM were aware of Presbyterians living in the border towns, there were no records. Other than word-of-mouth sharing of information, persons coming to minister on the border had no information to start with. "How does one explain to persons who have known only Roman Catholicism what a Presbyterian is?" asked Betty Martinez, who grew up in the "Lily of the Valleys" Presbyterian Church. Such was an early challenge to the Ministry.

When the Rev. Gary and Mrs. Beth Waller arrived, only providence could launch the ministry. (See outtake above.) Happily such things did happen but realizing the dreams was difficult. Eventually, the Rev. Luis and Mrs. Ana Lugo arrived to be the Mexican Co-coordinators with the Wallers. With the leadership on board, work could begin.

Rev. Lugo worked with Sister Amelia to begin having classes, studies, and worship services in her home and to acquire a lot for the church. Obtaining a lot meant navigating the Mexican bureaucracy. However, at last one was obtained and a fence erected. With the help of mission delegations, a building began to be built. Getting a permanent electrical pole installed required more cumbersome bureaucratic haggling within a system overwhelmed with new residents, businesses and factories, and many new, to Mexicans, strange churches.

México, at the time, operated most effectively with bribes. It was clear that a bribe would resolve the problem with the bureaucracy and get the church electricity, but Presbyterians considered bribes immoral. What to do? The neighbor was being kind, but stringing an extension cord was a cumbersome process each time there was a meeting and the church could not endure being thought of as a witches coven. (See Above p. 60). Finally, Sister Amelia resolved in her mind that a gift is not a bribe, so she offered the agent a case of beer. She explained that while she opposed drinking alcohol, it was up to the man whether he would drink it or not. The 'gift' worked.

Lily of the Valleys Church, Agua Prieta

As the work began with the congregation and its facilities, concern about finances developed. Oddly, the Wallers were placed without a funding source established and the ministry was having to pay everyone out of its own meager resources. That oversight was eventually corrected, but it raised an important issue of ongoing funding. By God's grace, Rev. Waller learned to be an effective fund raiser and reached out to congregations, presbyteries and synods for support and received a bountiful result.

Sister Amelia, Shirley Jewel and others saw the many needs of the people and began seeking contributions of food, clothing and medicines for the people of Agua Prieta. A small building was eventually built for that purpose alone and as time passed, the main building was expanded to include rooms for a medical and dental clinic, a kitchen and for a multi-purpose room that served as sanctuary, adult Sunday School, activities center, and dormitory for groups.

In the first years of the ministry, a focus was on building: the church building, the clothing closet, improvements to the church building eventually meeting a dream of Sister Amelia that the church would have a tile floor. Of course, repairs. Occasionally, groups would repaint the building inside and out and make repairs to the showers, evaporative coolers (air conditioning), and other improvements.

Fairly early an architect provided to the various ministries plans for small two room houses. In Agua Prieta, groups built six as a beginning. Four were provided to families and two were maintained for clinics in developing communities. Eventually, the one closest to the center of town was revised and incorporated into the pastor's home. The other became the nucleus for a grand community center in a neighborhood several miles from the church. It has become an important outreach to the community at large duplicating programs once offered at the church, such as: classes in hairdressing, cake decorating, sewing, and technology; a library; counseling and self-esteem classes, various children's programs, and so on to help families settle into and develop in a new environment.

Changes in personnel led to changes in vision for the work of FdC. The Wallers and Lugos were mostly focused on congregational development and meeting the incredible social needs of newly arriving migrants from the south. Besides those related directly to poverty were alcoholism among the men (see above), spousal abuse, abandonment, lack of pre-natal, birthing, and child care support for young women from their families who may as well have been a million miles away. (In the 80s phone service was lacking and cell phones and the internet did not exist). The ministry and church sought to fill the gaps.

New Church under Construction

Sister Amelia was constantly raising concerns about various needs, reported Betty Martínez, one of which was lack of water in the newer settlements. In response the ministry bought water tanks and a truck to deliver water to the people. This ministry continued until the mid 90s when the municipal government finally caught up with development and people could obtain a connection for a faucet in their yard which made life much easier.

In 1989, Les and Cathy Winters arrived as Co-coordinators. Les was an able former plant manager and Cathy an educator. While Les worked with groups and the continuing management of the ministry, Cathy went to work to try to meet a growing need by establishing a Child Care Center at the church. The government provided no child care since it had all it could do to provide elementary and secondary education for the children. In most cases both parents had to work and found it difficult to find jobs much less ones on opposite shifts. Many women found themselves single parents when their husbands crossed the border. The need for a safe and secure place for children was evident.

The center was a successful and important use of the church building that attracted much favorable attention from the community at large. However, as time passed, many services both municipal and corporate began to be developed which included child care facilities so the center closed down, a decision that shows the agility of Presbyterian Border Ministries in general. They readily begin ministries in times of need but willingly recognize when the need no longer exists and move on to other needs and concerns.

Another important need was health and dental care. So many of the migrants were unable to find jobs in the factories which meant they had no health insurance. Employers in México pay into the federal Social Security system which provides for retirement and for health care at the government hospitals. On the border, there were not enough jobs, so people often began a micro business to survive but did not have the income to pay the Social Security. FdC met this need through volunteer doctors and dentists, nurses and other health professionals but found it too sporadic. In the late 1980s the ministry began employing a doctor and a nurse to provide regular consultations at the church clinic and the two satellite clinics. The nurse built a network of health advocates who were trained to spot health concerns in the community and to educate others on nutrition and hygiene, pre and post natal care, and child care issues such as lactation and normal child development. Also, as the border became more developed and organized, medical and dental care became available so the ministry of health and dental care became less necessary and in less demand so the clinics ceased for the most part.

Under the leadership of the Rev. Jésus Gallegos, who arrived in Agua Prieta to replace the Lugos in 1992, the focus of FdC gradually moved from delegations doing work in the mornings and then vacationing in the afternoon resulting in only marginal engagement with the local Presbyterians. The ministry and delegations began to do Bible schools in cooperation with the church leadership and youth in various locations around the city and what are known as immersion experiences and opportunities for fellowship with the congregation of the church.

Immersion activities include learning about the realities behind the lives of the people in México. Rev. Gallegos did classes on the history of the Presbyterian Church within the context of the history of México.

Other persons in the ministry led groups on shopping trips to a local small grocery where they were required to shop on a Mexican family budget for a balanced diet for the family. Then they sought to help the delegation members understand the relative cost of their food budget to their income level. To have a healthy diet the average Mexican we learned would have to spend nearly 50 percent of their family income. Delegations often asked, "What about growing some of their own food?" The answer, "The desert is not an easy place to grow a garden."

As time has passed, the movement towards education, fellowship, and bible schools has grown. Today, FdC has also reached out to organizations working in drug and alcohol rehab, homelessness, technical education, community gardening, and migrant ministries done by other organizations and denominations building an ecumenical network previously unknown in México.

Under the leadership of the Rev. Mark Adams and the Rev. Gallegos and, following Rev. Gallegos, Elder José Ángel Valencia, the ministry moved towards intensive immersion experiences that engage delegations in understanding, not just the experience of those on the border, but also the issues and concerns that lead to immigration to the U.S. and understanding how difficult and dangerous it is to cross the border, what happens if a person gets caught, and the problems of migrants being deported back to México. In recent years FdC has been a major player in the development and staffing of the Migrant Resource Center that ministers to migrants who are deported. The ministry is housed in a building immediately next to the Mexican port of entry which enables persons to receive help with calling relatives, a sandwich, first aid for wounds not attended to by the Border Patrol, clothing, and directions to other services for homeless persons.

FdC has also become involved in advocacy for immigration reform and for a more humane Border Patrol joining "No More Deaths" and "Humane Borders"[25] in their work to provide water and first aid relief to persons crossing the desert of Arizona. Each week, FdC participates in a vigil on the U.S. side to memorialize the deaths of migrants who die crossing the border. The participants carry crosses with names and dates of the dead, every few feet one participant will lift the cross, cry out the name, and the other participants cry out, "Presente!", a commonly used word in Spanish. In essence we might say, "We lift you up!" or even "Lord, hear our prayer!" It is a moving and solemn experience.

After the turn of the millennium, members of the Lily of the Valleys Church, Eduardo Perez Verdugo and Daniel Cifuentes, who came from the coffee growing regions of México, began asking if there wasn't something that could be done with coffee. The discussion grew legs; Mark Adams had befriended a U.S. business manager, Tommy Bassett, and between them, the members of the church and others in the U.S. church a plan was hatched. A grant was written for a micro credit loan and Just Coffee was birthed. The story is told

---

[25] For the print media reader. No More Deaths may be found at: http://www.nomoredeaths.org and Humane Borders at http://www.humaneborders.org.

better in Just Coffee: Caffeine with a Conscience[26] by Mark Adams and Tommy Bassett. Just Coffee was envisioned as a cooperative effort between the farmers, the roaster/packers/marketing people in Agua Prieta and the churches in the U.S. where the coffee was to be sold. As of this writing Just Coffee is selling 60,000 pounds of coffee with increasing demand per year The project includes farm families from Chiapas, Nayarit, and Veracruz, six families in Agua Prieta who work in the roasting facility, and over a hundred churches and some businesses in the U.S. who sell the coffee.

The idea has grown into a model for economic development that can grow and expand, reduce the push of economics so that farm families can stay home and work together, family members can return home from the U.S., and the communities where the cooperatives are strengthened and developed. Since most of the workers in the roasting facilities are members of the Lily of the Valleys Church, the project has helped stabilize the church by stabilizing family income and giving cause to remain in Agua Prieta and the church.

Pueblos Hermanos—San Diego, California/ Tijuana, Baja California[27]

Pueblos Hermanos (PH) was founded soon after FdC and the Rev. William and Mrs. Susan Soldwisch,

---

[26] One can find more info on the book at http://www.justcoffee.org.

[27] Website: http://www.puebloshermanos.org. The following is gleaned from interviews with William Soldwisch, Juan Daniel Espitia, Robert Battenfield, Marta González Rojas, Nicassio Rojas, and Enrique Romero. For Baja Presbyterian Mission see: bajapresbyterianmissions.org.

were assigned by the Mission Board to work in San Diego and Tijuana. They arrived in June, 1984 tasked with beginning the process of forming a border ministry committee for the site. Their Mexican counterpart

Rev. Francisco Joachín,
President of Northwest Border

was Elder Juan Daniel Espitia (now a pastor of a Spanish language church nested in Solana Beach Presbyterian Church, Solana Beach, CA) came in 1985 serving until 1988 as Mexican Co-coordinator.

The work in Tijuana and Baja California did not have to be started from scratch because of the work of Baja Presbyterian Missions (BPM) Chartered in 1964 as Native Missions, a California Nonprofit Religious Corporation, it had been raising funds for years to fund churches and ministry in the region and was already working with Mexican pastors, mostly of Pentecostal background, to strengthen Protestant ministry in the Baja.

The Mexican Presbytery of the Northwest knew of the inactive facilities in the Aleman community formerly used by Project Concern, a ministry of Californians who found themselves unable to continue, and thought it could be a beginning. They sent Rev. Arturo Vázquez and his eleven children north to re-start the church which was renamed El Buen Pastor. The buildings were actually two houses that had been condemned for a new highway in San Diego, obtained by Presbyterians in San Diego and relocated to Tijuana.

When Rev. Vásquez reopened the work under the new name, people from the neighborhood flocked to the church expecting to be rewarded by handouts after the service. When that failed to happen, many ceased attending. The practice of giving out food, clothing, shoes, etc. was common among many missions but did not fit the INPM's view of evangelism, perhaps indicating a part of the problem that created the gap in thinking between INPM and PCUSA personnel and participants. Was health and social ministry just another form of hand outs?

The charge for the coordinators was to strengthen the present ministry and seek places to start new ones, especially to begin a new church in a middle class community so it could be a church that had the capacity to start new churches. Partly because of BPM, money for buildings was not an issue which made the ministry already more secure, and some funds were available for pastoral support. PH soon founded Dios Habla Hoy Church in the El Lago community of Tijuana under the leadership of Rev Espitia and Rev. Soldwisch. Once Rev. Enrique Romero arrived, succeeding Rev. Espitia as Mexican Co-coordinator, PH started La Nueva Vida, in El Pipila, Tijuana; and Dios Es Amor, in La Planecia, Tijuana.   NM/BPM contributed $45,000 toward construction of Dios Habla Hoy. In addition, PH and

NM/BPM jointly developed Dios Con Nosotros, in Otay/Universidad, Tijuana. First buying and adding a second story to an unfinished building (manse upstairs), and later BPM provided $180,000 to fund construction of an adjoining two-story sanctuary with off-street parking beneath.

Of course, one task the Soldwisches faced that the Wallers did not was finding a way to work with BPM and the already existing work in México. Rev. Vásquez and his congregation and those under his leadership were the easier task as the INPM is notably Episcopal in nature, meaning that more authority is lodged with the presbyteries and the General Assembly than is the case in the PCUSA. (Interview with Dr. Pazos). The center of power and decision is in the governing board (junta) in México City. Once the General Assembly spoke, the presbyters (pastors) and presbyteries were expected to obey. When the INPM made the decision to participate in the border ministries, Rev. Vásquez was expected to participate. He was inclined to do so anyway as Tijuana was on the far northwest edge of México and the closest Mexican Presbyterian pastor was hundreds of mile away. With the beginning of PBM he hoped to have colleagues soon with whom he could work and fellowship.

Mr. Espitia arrived less than a year after the Soldwisches and the work became more extensive, especially getting the binational ministry established and building an understanding of its goals. Both Mr. Espitia and the Soldwisches report that the relationships between them began and continued to be quite good. Mr. Espitia's work in translating for an international evangelism project meant he knew English and spoke it well, had worked an ecumenical environment, and had a grasp of U.S. culture. Rev. William and Susan Soldwisch (from the Philippines) were already engaged in cross cultural relationship in their marriage and knew Spanish quite well. Communication was easier and translation for meetings far better than many locations. Even Rev. Enrique Romero, who followed Mr. Espitia, had considerable international experience and mission work outside of México. Many of the challenges to border ministry regarding culture and language were easier to deal with as a result of these backgrounds.

One immediate challenge was working with the differences of viewpoint between the vision of Presbyterian Border Ministry, Baja Presbyterian Missions and Native Missions (NM) founded by Roland and Kay Taylor, elders of La Jolla Presbyterian Church. They had begun the work of BPM in their church by raising funds through an annual festival for one project or the other in México. BPM was started as a means to engage other churches and individuals in the work. When the Soldwisches arrived, BPM was mostly working with Mexican ministers to strengthen old or start new Protestant churches which were mostly Pentecostal. Rev. Soldwisch had the responsibility of interpreting the vision of PBM to Baja Missions. Through conversations and prayer Mr. Taylor and his board came to recognize the possibilities and decided to support the work despite having a slightly different vision. Indications of the spirit of cooperation between the various entities is indicated by persons like Mr. Bob Battenfield, an elder at at Fletcher Hills Presbyterian Church, who joined the NM Board in 1988 about the same time he joined PBM's

Corporate Board, which was tasked with fundraising for work along the border. Rev. Tom Erickson, former pastor at Fletcher Hills and a PBM Corporate Board member, recruited Mr. Battenfield to help with marketing PBM to potential donors.

There was, of course, the Presbytery of San Diego, the Synod of the Southwest, INPM's Northwest Presbytery and others to gather into the work. The Synod and Presbytery were both strong supporters of the beginning of PBM and readily lent their support. However, as several attested, every new idea stimulates a thousand different understandings, so Rev. Soldwisch had to lead the many possible players to a common vision.

The PCUSA saw the work as having to include social ministry, an aspect Susan Soldwisch was suited for but one BPM was less in agreement with. BPM leaned towards the Mexican viewpoint on the subject of evangelism and church planting and was less interested in social concerns. However, once the work in health ministry proceeded the value of the work was recognized as a means to evangelism, especially, with the employment of Marta González Rojas. She was a nurse who sacrificed a very good position with the government health care system to join the PH delegation and Dr. Jorge Pazos to provide more extensive health services. Both saw their work as a means to sharing their faith which they faithfully did. Also, instead of giving away clothing and food as enticement to worship services, the social programs were working during the week to provide much needed health care and other services, intentionally sharing their faith as they did. As Señora González said,

> We did consultations and examinations, taught classes on hygiene, birth control, sexuality, infant care, self-esteem, drug addiction, sexually transmitted diseases, and nutrition, but always read the Bible, prayed, invited people to accept Christ. Many times someone would be in crisis and we would call a pastor or elder to come and counsel with them. We always said, 'Marta did not do this, the church did not do this, God did this. All we do is because God loves you and wants for you a good and healthy life. We do not heal you, Jesus does.'

Since training pastors is a long time process and many pastors from the south did not want to live in the north (the same kinds of prejudices based on rumor exist in México as in the U.S. between regions), especially hearing of the heat of the desert, the ministry tried to use lay ministers. Their first experiences did not turn out well. One of the lay pastors was terrible at interpersonal relations and nearly killed a promising ministry. Two others were guilty of sexual misconduct casting a pall on the Presbyterians. PH contacted the Presbytery of Northwest and the INPM Council to request a pastor. A pastor was appointed and sent with a short term commitment. Once he arrived he decided to stay in the north. He worked with three churches and eventually more pastors were recruited to the north making possible more extensive and supporting work to be done. The churches from Ensenada, Mexicali, and

Tijuana began having regular meetings of young people in the various locations to do evangelistic activities on behalf of the churches.

Because Tijuana is close to a large U.S. population center, a lot of differing church groups were doing work in Tijuana often with little or no knowledge of what others were doing. While for the most part this created no problems, it often led to new wrinkles. For example, in 1986 a Korean missionary, Rev. Lee, came to work in Tijuana under the auspices of one of the Presbyterian churches in Korea. He spent about six months getting

familiar with the landscape and then began developing his own ministry. He founded two churches, Mt. Sion and Mt. Sian, whose leadership came from new seminary graduates. The plan for these churches to become established in four years dragged out to many more, but eventually they were turned over to the Mexican Presbytery. Needless to say, as the Korean initiative proceeded, there was another Presbyterian ministry that could be brought into the work of PH, ignored, or, at minimum, be a cooperating partner.

PH worked on cooperation and, as mission delegations began to arrive, they went to help out in churches of PH and the Korean ministry which led to good relations between all with a few exceptions. The Koreans never understood the INPM's opposition to giving gifts to attract attendance at worship services, a practice common in Korea. The Korean missionaries learned well the lessons of U.S. mission workers and had decidedly paternalistic attitudes.

Many Presbyterian churches in the U.S. would be pleased to have the Dios Es Amor Presbyterian Church building(see photos). Its sanctuary is large enough to hold several hundred persons. It includes numerous meeting rooms, modern electricity, bathrooms, and electronic equipment. The Pastor, Rev. Beimar Santizo, said that the vision of the Koreans was that the buildings would be a conference center much like they have in Korea where evangelism conferences, youth conventions, and, possibly, one day a seminary could be housed. Problem? The Mexican problems include the distances between the churches, cost of lodging and the fact that few Mexican Presbyterians are middle class much less rich. Sadly, the pastor reports, "The building for classes often has more pigeons and doves than people on Sunday." (There are windows but, instead of glass, some windows were constructed using designer blocks which have spaces through which the birds can enter.)

As we toured the facility, I looked out a window in a stairwell to see an incredible mountain vista. I wondered aloud why the sanctuary nor any of the rooms was built with a window looking out over the mountain scene. The pastor only lamented, "They did not think of that."

In PBM, as in all of church life, providential things happen that change what is done. A Phoenix church once asked if the health ministry could use a mobile home for its work. PH responded that it could and asked for something at most thirty feet long. Moving trailers around Tijuana and locating them on the lots made available is not always an easy task. It is a mountainous city with many steep climbs and sharp curves. Instead, the church found a fifty foot construction trailer for free, outfitted it, and informed the ministry they would bring it down when arrangements for crossing it were made. Dr. Pazos made arrangements and got it across for $45.00, a miracle in itself that could not happen today. The trailer was named "Salud y Vida" (Health and Life) and placed in a squatters[28] neighborhood to begin work there out of which grew a church. At times moving the trailer to a new site was challenging to say the least.

The Rojases consider the health ministry to have been an important vehicle for bringing the gospel to the people of Tijuana. It has given U.S. Presbyterians an opportunity to share their expertise and their love with people who badly need it. They say that whenever the Presbyterians of the U.S. come and interact so directly with the poor in the neighborhoods, especially the squatters communities, both the mission delegations and the people served feel the presence of God.

When asked what was the most important gift of PH, every interviewee responded, "The relationships." All the Mexicans admit that the money and material contributions matter, but that they don't talk about that much when a delegation leaves or they dedicate a new building. What does get discussed is always the brothers and sisters in Christ they have made. Even U.S. Presbyterians who have served respond likewise. My daughter, Kimberly, served at PH the summer of 1992. She told me, "Marta is the reason I decided to go to medical school. I was thinking of being a minister, and she showed me a way to minister through medicine."

Rev. Romero spoke of the importance of the many relationships and ways in which PH was able to live in a symbiotic relationship with the other players. Baja

---

[28] Squatter is not used to stigmatize. It is a common term for the new neighborhoods that developed to the outsider in a haphazard fashion. However, with thousands of persons migrating to the cities for work and, especially to the north, such neighborhoods of new residents who simply move onto a lot and begin life is common.

Missions altered its approach to work in the Baja in order to lend its support to the work of PH, the PCUSA partners came to see the integral link between social ministry and church planting, and all players welcomed the Korean missionary endeavors despite there being some cultural differences that created friction. However, as time has passed the trinational nature of the work has led to important successes. Today, several churches are strong and existing in middle class communities and able to lend support in other directions. While the Presbytery of Northwest Border has grown to nearly twenty missions and/or churches with nearly as many pastors, it is far from self-sufficient and sustaining. The support that comes from the U.S. is essential to the ongoing success of PH and the INPM in the Baja. Delegations that come from churches far and wide in the U.S. are a great help to the development of a strong Presbyterian Church in México for health and social ministry, Bible Schools that reach the children of the community, repairs to facilities, and, most important, for the building of relationships between the Mexican and U.S. Presbyterians.

Pasos de Fe—El Paso, Texas/Ciudad Juárez, Chihuahua[29]

Pasos de Fe is unique among Presbyterian border ministries because it could claim to be the first such ministry. However, as indicated previously, its predecessor ministry Proyecto Verdad founded in 1973 collapsed in 1989 over a personnel dispute between the

[29] Pasos de Fe has no website.

Mexican leadership and the U.S. leadership mentioned elsewhere. One possible reason for the conflict may be the legacy of the goals of Proyecto Verdad, representing

Principe de La Paz Church

the older paternalistic model that conflicted with the goals of Presbyterian Border Ministry. While a first of its kind for the U.S. Presbyterians, it had to be absorbed by PBM which took a while and some transformation.

The project was founded once Rev. Hugh D. Nelson, who had been a missionary to México, became the Executive Presbyter of Synod of the Sun. In that position, he and his colleagues in the synods and presbyteries began to develop a concern for and a plan for a ministry in Ciudad Juárez, indeed for the whole of the border regions. That vision was to provide a holistic ministry that would provide both the social needs of the people of the city through health care, clothing, food, and various kinds of classes and services, and the spiritual needs through the founding of churches in Juárez. While PV focused on social needs, churches were also founded adding support and energy to the church Príncipe de Paz which had been founded in 1965. During the following decades, several more Presbyterian churches were founded. The motivation for these churches came primarily from the U.S. The involvement of INPM came later illustrating the continuing paternalism in mission work despite the considerable wisdom of Rev. Nelson in leading the project.[30]

Pasos del Norte, later renamed El Paso when it passed into U.S. hands after the Mexican American War, was an old Mexican city founded in 1659 by Spanish Franciscan priests.[31] The town was located on the most passable ford of the Rio Grande resulting in its name "The Pass". After it changed hands and was renamed, the U.S. developed Ft. Bliss, an army base, near the town and the town grew as a result of the extra stimulus of the military.

By the 1960s Juárez and El Paso were growing. Juárez sought to develop into an industrial center that led to the development of numerous factories and many thousands of new residents. As with the border in general, Juárez developed all the problems of such rapid growth and development. Being one of the earliest border cities to develop, Juárez and the federal government were less prepared than in other border communities for dealing with the development. By 2006 over 200,000 persons were employed in factories almost

---

[30] Interview with William Soldwisch.

[31] Except where noted the following paragraphs are gleaned from the 2006 publication of the Mission Team Manual for Pasos de Fe.

all having arrived in recent years from other parts of México.

Growth in Juárez stimulated growth in El Paso. Presbyterians in the U.S. had many churches, two of which were Spanish language churches. El Paso was and is overwhelmingly Mexican. Given the strong presence of Presbyterians in El Paso, it was a natural location for a cross border ministry. As time passed almost all the churches in Juárez had Mexican leadership some of whom had been trained by the mission leadership of Synod of the Sun. Others were recruited from other parts of México.

Evidently, with the failure of the ministry in 1989, time passed before a new attempt could be started. The personnel issues were a learning experience and the crisis in Proyecto Verdad and similar, but less costly ones, at Puentes del Cristo and Proyecto Amistad (Piedras Negras) at almost the same time led to a study and development of personnel procedures.[32] Especially, since the work at Proyecto Verdad and Puentes de Cristo were the oldest and most mature, the crisis was a good example for bringing out an issue that was bound to affect the newer ministries if not recognized and corrected. The relationships and backgrounds of the leadership at Pueblos Hermanos (see above) demonstrated some of the qualities most important to strong, consistent leadership and project development as discussed elsewhere. PV and PdC struggled with leadership that was unable to grapple effectively with the

---

[32] Minutes of the Committee of Presbyterian Border Ministry, August 28-29, 1989)

attempt to overcome paternalism which led to a conflict with the model of binational ministry.

Despite the crisis and the withdrawal of the Mexican partners at PV, few lost sight of the need for a binational ministry of Presbyterians in Ciudad Juárez and El Paso. In fact, evidence indicates a cordial and informal relationship for the ensuing years between pastors and elders in México and the U.S., however, the breathing room gave time to heal and the work going on in other parts of the frontier gave hope that a new ministry could begin. So in 1998 the new ministry was begun under the auspices of Presbyterian Border Ministry and named Pasos de Fe with the goal "to serve the immediate El Paso/Juárez area, but also the entire extent of the presbyteries of Tres Ríos (western Texas), Sierra Blanca (southern and eastern New México) and Chihuahua (North-Central México)."[33]

The ministry presently includes two churches in Ciudad Chihuahua and eight churches or missions in Ciudad Juárez mostly served by energetic pastors. One of the longest serving pastors of a single church is the Rev. Baltazar González at Renovación in Juárez and a major contributor to the work of PBM. Today, most of the pastors are young adults coming from other regions of the country. Their commitment to the development of the older churches and the founding of new ones is evident. However, a continued recognition that social ministry leads to opportunities of evangelism, Pastors Roberto Mendoza and Mercedes Romo Castro work to keep the community center in western Juárez alive and

---

[33] Manual, p.10.

developing with classes for women and children, a computer lab, a library, tutoring, and evangelism classes.

In 2011 Rev. Romo accepted a position at low pay to have an official position to work part time as the director of the community center that makes him *de facto* Mexican coordinator of Pasos de Fe. At this writing, the ministry is being operated much like a church that has lost its pastoral staff in which the session must do the work according to the Rev. John Nelsen, pastor of University Presbyterian Church in El Paso and president of the boards of both PdF and Presbyterian Border Ministry. As a church session leads the work of the church when it lacks a pastor, the binational committee is responsible for keeping PdF going."The challenges are great", says Nelsen, "because we've lacked a consistent leadership in the ministry. We've had wonderful people, but they've been nearly volunteers with short term commitments. To build Pasos de Fe, we need long term leadership which is why Frontera, Pueblos Hermanos and Amistad have done well and the other ministries are suffering."[34]

Mendoza and Romo give another reason. "Since the violence has risen here in Juárez, we no longer have mission delegations. The support from them was instrumental in our continuing to do the ministry. It's not just their work at building and repairs, Bible Schools, and health clinics. They also paid a registration fee that helped support the ministry." (Most of the PBM sites asked a registration fee for each delegation member to cover the costs of receiving the delegations on the border and working with them. The delegations also

---

[34] Interview with Rev. John Nelsen. See below for a discussion of the transition from Presbyterian Border Ministry to Presbyterian Border Region Outreach.

paid the costs of materials for whatever work they did. An estimate of costs had to be made up front and paid so that the money could be exchanged and deposited in the accounts of the ministries in México. Often the delegations donated whatever remained of their deposits for materials or made up whatever deficit may occur.)

Rev. Nelsen reported that PdF lacked funds even to pay Romo Castro for his work. However, Romo Castro is committed to the work and offered to work for a very small stipend so he could justify his time with the Presbytery. The salary, as small as it is, also represents an investment of the Pasos de Fe board in the work and ownership over it.

One of the innovative ways Pasos de Fe is seeking to minister to the community is to hold a rabies clinic at the community center which is still located in a very poor neighborhood. For those of us living in a developed nation that is largely middle class, rabies only crosses our minds when we take our pets to the veterinarian. We are also aware that there are rabies clinics where our less affluent neighbors may have their pets vaccinated. Our only concern with rabies is with wild animals who only occasionally invade our neighborhoods bringing rabies, but because our pets are vaccinated we need only worry about direct contact with humans. However, in the large cities of México, sanitation services are lacking especially in poorer neighborhoods; trash builds up and attracts rats from the countryside; the rats bring rabies, the cats attack the rats which bite at the cats who contract rabies. The cats and dogs live in close proximity and it is not unusual for a cat, especially a rabid one, to bite a dog thus infecting it. Needless to say living in a world where there are rabies infected animals is frightening.

"There is no way to stop the rats that we can do anything about," said Rev. Romo Castro, "nor can we catch all the cats because many are wild. We can only protect the dogs which families consider essential for protecting their house. [NOTE: the dogs are an alarm system for those in the house.] So we have a veterinarian friend who agreed to give the vaccines. All we had to do is pay him his cost for the medication." The day of the clinic about fifty dogs arrived early and the people waited for over an hour for the vet to arrive. In the end about one-hundred dogs were vaccinated and many opportunities for ministry had occurred. As they waited, the people received flyers telling of the other ministries of the Community Center and Pasos de Fe. Many of the participants who were there gladly shared the importance of the vaccinations and told me that they

believed that Pasos de Fe was demonstrating the love of God for them and their pets.

It is impossible to discuss the ministries on the México/Texas border without addressing violence which is far more intense in that region than it has been in Sonora, the state where Agua Prieta and Nogales are located.[35] Juárez has witnessed some of the most serious and egregious acts of violence anywhere with much of it aimed at women, including a massacre commemorated with a cross at the border that displays a railroad tie spike for each woman murdered. (Photo) Some people believe some women were victims of a serial killer, but at least one mass burial site was found which bore the marks of a mass killing. The violence against women is tragic and so is the violence that daily takes lives often in compelling acts meant to send a signal. Most often it is clear the violence is to warn off a political figure, a business person or a competitor in drugs and human trafficking. As the Rev. Juan Pablo Gutiérrez said, "The violence is targeted. The general public is in danger when a battle breaks out in an area where one happens to be." However, I was startled when he met me at a park near the border and told me, "We are going to drive at thirty kilometers per hour unless we are stopped by a traffic light. We will stop but if we see guns, we will go ahead as quickly as possible." Thanks be to God, we saw no evidence of weapons except when a military vehicle passed us. "The average visitor to Juárez is safe as we are unless we walk into violence. They are not interested in bothering us. Their interest is their business."

---

[35] I do not wish to minimize that Nogales has traditionally been a violent city especially at night, see more on Nogales and violence below.

A common problem that affects the ministry of Pasos de Fe and the churches that seek to help the poor is intimidation by gangs not necessarily under the control of the cartels. The gangs extort the business owners for protection money. The costs are often high. Bernice Gutiérrez Sichler, a dentist, closed her practice because she did not believe paying the protection fees were morally right. Later, she was forced to close the clinic operated at Príncipe de Paz Church because of the threat and because as a free clinic, she and the ministry could not afford to pay.

As Rev. Nelsen had testified and Rev. Romo affirmed, the violence has hurt the ministry by scaring off the mission delegations. As Pastor Mendoza said, "The delegations have every right to be concerned about the violence. Nobody can bring a delegation without that concern. We believe that it is possible to come to Juárez and never see any violence. Several of us have only seen its results, not been in the actual place. You have been here a week and not seen any actual violence. For the most part the city is safe, but the danger lurks." Juan Pablo Gutiérrez spoke in similar terms and added, "We live in a good neighborhood and a nice house but we have often heard automatic gunfire so it is a worry. Thanks be to God none of us has been caught in the middle of it. We wouldn't want that to happen to any visitors from the U.S."

Two years later, 2014, the violence had subsided a great deal in Juárez and other parts of México. That does not mean the worry is over, but perhaps it is waning. I address the present circumstances in the next part.

Puentes de Cristo— McAllen, Texas/Reynosa, Tamaulipas[36]

I regret that I was never able to visit or to interview persons with PdC because as the second border ministry begun before PBM was actually started it plays an important role in the history of Border Ministry. However, the realities of the ministry made it impossible for them to receive me and to arrange for interviews. Readers may visit their website to discover more about PdC. I have indicated its role in PBM in other places and the work it does continues to contribute to the kingdom of God. Below, I have provided the highlights from the ministry's website.

Having been founded in 1981 by a group of pastors from the Rio Grand River Valley, PdC sought to provide ministry on both sides of the border on a binational

---

[36] Website: http://www.puentesdecristo.org

model, therefore, the board was made up characteristically of representatives from both sides. A number of ministries quickly followed, including churches, medical clinics, after school, nutrition, and self-development programs. From its early days until recent years, a major component of the ministry was inviting and facilitating mission delegations from U.S. churches.

Today, PdC is focusing on:

- developing opportunities for fellowship and celebration between the Anglo and Hispanic communities in Hidalgo, TX, working with First Presbyterian Church of McAllen and Mission Presbytery;
- evangelism through work with children and their families in a neighborhood of Reynosa;
- self-development projects helping women become self-sufficient through learning to be seamstresses and cosmetologists;
- ministry to hispanics in McAllen through prayer and Bible study groups;
- new church development seeking to plant seeds from growth on both sides of the border in hopes of forming new churches.

Since 2008, PdC has undergone a reassessment of their ministry under the guidance of PCUSA Mission co-workers the Rev. and Mrs. Andres Garcia and the board. The reassessment sought to understand ministry on the border in light of "the impact of globalization on the provincial life of the border including crisis of security and prolonged state of war against terrorism and drug trafficking, and finally the deficit of trust and loss of credibility of dominant religious organizations." (See website note 35).

As the website suggests, PdC looks forward in hope to a new era in its ministry.

Proyecto Amistad—
Laredo, Texas/Nuevo Laredo, Tamaulipas[37]

Victoria en Jesucristo Church

Present day Proyecto Amistad is a merger of two ministries begun in 1985 under the auspices of Presbyterian Border Ministry. The original Proyecto Amistad was located in Piedras Negras, Coahuila, MX and Eagle Pass, TX, USA. Laredos Unidos was established in Nuevo Laredo, Tamaulipas, MX and Laredo, TX, USA about the same time. The two had similar missions to satisfy the concerns of both the

---

[37] Website: http://www.proyectoamistad.org/about-us/. Except where indicated the following is the result of interviews with Roberto Medina, Susan Frerichs, and Chris McReynolds the co-coordinators of Proyecto Amistad.

Mexican and U.S. Presbyterians. Mexican pastors were recruited and hired in 1986 to begin evangelistic work and establish a mission that would one day become a church. Work began also with personnel from the U.S. to provide health ministries and other humanitarian assistance.

The missions were easy to start because there were a few Presbyterians already identified and other interested families who were meeting in homes. Almost immediately after the pastors arrived, a search began for a suitable place for a space dedicated to the mission and land was purchased before the end of 1986. Laredos Unidos had an advantage because a church, Puerta del Cielo, had been in existence since 1965, was a healthy congregation and lent moral support to the work of the new missionaries.

In 1988, Proyecto Amistad had purchased additional property for the community center and a home for the pastor, Rev. Jesse González, which led to many possibilities for ministry including the expansion of the health ministries and other social outreach programs to the community. Laredos Unidos was engaged in a similar time line and track.

Rev. González was described by a former parishioner as dynamic and charismatic who made the Bible come alive. The woman began taking her children to church once she had met him. She and each of the children became Christians and then her husband also. Such is the story one hears from all.

The family of Sandra Murrillo in Piedras Negras bore witness to the importance of the social ministries of Proyecto Amistad in their lives and faith. On April 4,

2004, there had been a terrible flood in the city resulting from a heavy rain several miles upstream. Despite their house being located about twenty feet above the normal river level, the flood broke down on them by surprise. They barely escaped, but their house did not. "Everything was destroyed, or nearly so. Our house, clothes, car, and animals— all gone. Thanks be to God, Señor Medina and the others at the church and Amistad helped us. People came from the U.S. to help build our house and help us reclaim the property. They were so kind and sacrificed so much for my family, thanks be to God. Now we are settled and are able to have our family

with us," she said sweeping her hand to indicate the children and grandchildren around her.

Nieves, another woman in the community, told of the visit of one mission delegation for which she prepared a meal. The delegation came and ate her tacos until none was left. Several commented on how wonderful they were and wanted to know how she made them. They looked incredulous when she told them the meat was rat meat, hardly believable for people from the U.S. "Where do you get them?" asked one delegation member. "We go to the farm and catch them. The farmers appreciate it." And to the surprise of the delegation, she offered to take them on a rat hunt. The next day the delegation hunted rats, butchered them and prepared another meal. Her way of ministering to the delegation that had been ministering to her and her neighbors was with a cross cultural and mind expanding experience. "I think it was the first time that Christians from the U.S. knowingly thanked God for a dinner made with rats," she said with a laugh. Indeed! But such are the experiences of those involved in mission—they learn new things about God's creation including that the much maligned rat is a gift from God and good to eat.

After several years, one church had been started in Piedras Negras and a mission in Ciudad Acuña, while in Nuevo Laredo several missions were created in the new neighborhoods and work progressed steadily. A community center was built and health ministries, a child care center, and programs to assist the poor and classes designed to support and encourage the women were soon underway. In both cities, the work was progressing well with the aid of mission delegations from the U.S. and the energy of the Mexican co-coordinators, pastors, and church members.

Then there were personnel changes. Rev. González left to go to seminary. U.S. coordinators changed and in Piedras Negras a crisis similar to that with Proyecto Verdad and Puentes de Cristo occurred resulting in

David Cassie, U.S. Co-coordinator, stating at that time that "in my opinion, the assignment process is not adequate, inasmuch as it does not show up the differences of temperament or work style upon which will depend a harmonious climate." (Minutes, PBM Committee, August 28-29, 1989). Having learned from that earlier crisis, the board of Amistad reacted differently to the crisis than did that of Proyecto Verdad and a total collapse was averted.

The ensuing years saw many changes, but with the commitments of churches from the U.S. and the encouragement of the Presbytery of the Northeast in México, the two ministries survived although the church in Piedras Negras found itself plateauing after Rev. González resigned as pastor, but he continued as Mexican Co-coordinator. Susan Frerichs explained that the pastor who followed Rev. González never worked without his predecessors shadow, "the church members were not from the community where the church was located. Then a series of church members divorced each other, others left for the U.S. or other places in México. But one problem was the church, which was mostly middle class and living in other parts of the city, never knew how to minister in the community which had drug and alcohol addiction, prostitution and youth gangs." For a while the community center continued to serve a good purpose and absorbed much of the time and energy of the Mexican coordinator, who also had responsibility for the church. The arrangement often created stress and negotiation of commitments on the part of the Mexican coordinators who were receiving far less income than their U.S. counterpart. There was always a struggle over the issues of pay equity when the Mexican coordinator thought he had far more to do than the U.S. coordinator.

Changing leadership at Amistad and other ministries was a problem because it takes several years to grow comfortable with the context, one's working partners, and with the many details of the ministry. Sadly, long term leadership was lacking on either side of the border partly because, as one person told me, "the border context sort of chews you up and spits you out."

Amistad was blessed in 1995 to have Susanne Frerich, an intern, come from college to serve the ministry. She served in the role of co-coordinator of Amistad for nearly twelve years, having transitioned from intern to co-coordinator. During her service the ministries of both Amistad and Laredos Unidos prospered with numerous mission delegations coming to assist in the work. However, many changes occurred that would result in transformation of the two. The borderlands were always changing.

First, as in other places, México was able to develop better national and local resources to meet the needs of the people of Piedras Negras and Nuevo Laredo including better health care, improved water and electrical distributions, a growing education network, and other government services that most U.S. citizens take for granted. The results were that the needs for a number of the ministries declined to the point that it was unwise to continue the ministries.

Second, the terrorist attack on the World Trade Center, Pentagon of September 11, 2001 happened resulting in the hardening of the border with additional security at the ports of entry causing longer crossing times in both directions, but exponentially so for those seeking entry to or re-entry to the U.S. Because the security procedures were increased prior to developing adequate infrastructure and personnel, the wait times to re-enter the U.S. grew to hours instead of minutes.

In addition, U.S. citizens grew fearful of traveling at all and security conscious people felt greater reticence to travel into México, a place many already considered dangerous. With the hardening of the border, organized crime entered the human migration picture helping to fund their operations with another income source and providing them a larger transportation system because they exploited those who wished to cross. (See below regarding systems for crossing migrants).

So the third change taking place on the border was a definite increase in violence. (See charts in Part III: Chapter 1.) As news of the escalating violence reached Presbyterians in the U.S., they began canceling already planned trips or not even considering México's borderlands and PBM ministries as possible places to take mission delegations. While it is unlikely that a mission delegation would be targeted and the violence is seemingly random in terms of where it happens, Mexican co-coordinator Roberto Medina said, "Even now that the violence has subsided, I would not feel comfortable with a group larger than three or four persons who could travel with me in my car. A caravan is too dangerous because we could not easily escape a gun fight if we happened into one."

Mr. Medina has himself been the victim of a number of robberies so that he no longer carries money with him and he travels less in the rural areas. He persists in his work that requires him to travel on occasion to distant cities where Amistad now supports churches and programs. His commitment to his work is courageous because he could go back to his private business and his job with the Revenue Service of México and Kassumy, his wife, could return to nursing, far more lucrative than serving Amistad. As she told Roberto when he began to consider his call to Amistad, "You can't do this half way. It's all or nothing. Full time or no time." They continue to share their commitment full time.

All these changes colluded to require the closing of the Amistad Presbyterian Center in 2001. And later the center in Nuevo Laredo, and eventually the merging of the two ministries into one with the name Proyecto Amistad on January 1, 2007. At one time both centers were providing two doctors and two nurses, a dining room to provide full meals for children, training for health promoters and other vocational training. Decisions to end such work were difficult to make, but needs had changed and the ministry saw it had to look to the future not try to maintain unnecessary work and commitments of time and energy. Without delegations on a regular basis the finances were becoming a greater concern as donations tended to dry up when mission delegations no longer experienced the needs personally.

By the time decisions were made to close ministries and merge Amistad with Laredos Unidos, both Frerichs and Medina had been serving together since Medina first served on the board of Amistad in 1996 and began volunteering in the ministry. The consistency and the historical understanding, awareness of the communities, and their ties to the churches and presbyteries in the U.S. helped them guide the ministries to re-envision the future and to focus their resources more effectively. It is not clear that the decision to merge and move Medina and the offices of the merged ministry to Nuevo Laredo had any actual affect on the church in Piedras Negras, but it soon closed for lack of adequate leadership and congregation.

When Frerichs left Amistad, Medina's presence was instrumental in aiding a smooth transition with Elder Chris McReynolds who had also been a volunteer with PBM for some time and knew the ministry from that perspective. It was one of those happy transitions.

The decisions leading to the merger responded to frustrations common to PBM ministries. As Ms. Frerichs explained: "The Mexicans wanted more emphasis and money for church development. The PCUSA partners were often impatient that the Mexicans were not engaging in the health and social ministries very much. In fact, all the personnel was Mexican thus providing their gifts, knowledge and skills. Often the PCUSA moved ahead with ministries the Mexican pastors and churches were not interested in pursuing. While not a huge conflict, there was often the discomfort that the PCUSA which was providing the money, asserted itself and imposed its will on the Mexican partners."

When funds became more scarce decisions had to be made. By 2005 the need for a medical ministry was clearly waning. A survey was done in Piedras Negras that found the needs for medical and dental services were no longer what was being provided. Instead, the people needed much more sophisticated medical and dental care that the ministry could not provide. The boards of both ministries were aware that the two ministries were serving the same region as both expanded deeper into México.

The question had to be asked whether economy of personnel and finances did not demand a major change. Finally, in 2006 the two boards decided to transition to one ministry that would be located in Laredo and Nuevo Laredo but take the name of Proyecto Amistad, an obvious compromise to honor the partnership and avoid

La Hermosa Church, Caborca

the appearance that they were just closing down Amistad. The board also decided to focus its attention on church development and study what social needs they could address. See below for the response of Proyecto Amistad to recent border conditions.

Compañeros en Misión—
Nogales, Arizona/Nogales, Sonora[38]

Compañeros en Misión was founded in 1993 with the name Nogalhillos combining the names of Nogales and Hermosillo. In 1999 the name of the ministry was changed to Compañeros en Misión. When I first visited the Ambos Nogales (both Nogales) in May 1995, the Rev. Bill Buehler and his wife, Marge, had been appointed as the U.S. coordinators. There was no Mexican coordinator yet.

The plan was for the Buehlers, who had served at Frontera de Cristo for an interim period and in other parts of Latin America, to start a worshipping community. They hoped to have a Bible study going in a couple of locations in Nogales, Sonora by one year and mission churches by the end of the second or third year. God had another plan.

Two sets of brothers who had been serving as Methodist pastors in Hermosillo, Caborca, Magdalena, Guaymas, Navojoa and Nogales, had become discouraged because they had little in the way of spiritual or material support from Methodists (The 1914 plan of Cincinnati had designated northern México to be Methodist territory as it did southern México to be Presbyterian). The brothers had few other Methodist pastors in the region and approached the Buehlers about working on theirm becoming Presbyterians. For all concerned it seemed a good idea. For them, the

---

[38] CeM does not have a website. I depend here on a number of Interviews which took place in Tucson, Nogales, Hermosillo and Caborca.. I will simply indicate the persons with whom I spoke.

Presbyterians were establishing a front with well trained workers in the Buehlers, work had progressed in Agua Prieta and Tijuana so other pastors for emotional and spiritual support were not terribly far away. For Presbyterians, it meant the work could take a great leap forward. The four brothers were trained in Presbyterian ways and worked into the INPM.

The partnership worked for a while, but after several years the two sets of brothers left, and it was up to the INPM and Presbytery of Chihuahua to continue the work. Sadly, neither had the capacity to place prepared leadership at each site. Eventually, they had to close the sites in Guaymas and Navojoa in 2007 because of the lack of leadership.

Young "obreros" (lay pastors) were assigned to serve the missions in Caborca, Magdalena, Hermosillo and Nogales. After some time, CeM was able to provide resources for their seminary education. The young men were energetic and sought to serve well, but the work was overwhelming and the climate, especially in Caborca, oppressive. Although the work faltered, it continued and a community center was built in Hermosillo and partnerships were developed in Nogales to provide for more or less similar programs of health ministries, breakfast and lunch programs for children, clothing and food closets, and vocational and educational programs.

Despite the reputation of Nogales as a violent city, delegations from the U.S still made pilgrimages. Building housing in some squatters communities, the community center in Hermosillo, churches and lives were transformed.[39] I spoke with women in Caborca, and men in Hermosillo who testified to the difference the Presbyterians had made in their lives by teaching them the gospel. Families torn by drugs and alcohol and family violence have experienced salvation and completely changed lives. Many have benefitted from the health ministry and self-esteem classes. Through their relationship with the church and with Christ their lives have stabilized, their children grown healthy and confident, and, of great importance to many, have been provided support against entering the world of drugs, alcohol and violence.

Voz del Desierto Church, Hermosillo

Pastors Roberto Mendoza and Mercedes Romo Castro, now serving in Ciudad Juárez, were products of the ministry of Compañeros. Both had a history of alcohol and drug abuse and became involved in ministry through the drug and alcohol treatment programs of the ministry. They went on to attend seminary and enter the

---

[39] See Above: "Differing Perspectives"

ministry. Once they completed seminary they returned to Sonora where they worked with churches and with Compañeros before moving on to Juárez. One layman commented, "Every day I wake up without a hangover I see the work of Jesus in my life and thank him for the Presbyterians who introduced me to him and helped me get off alcohol."

Health education has been a ministry of importance since few of the people have access to teaching about proper hygiene, nutrition, blood pressure, diabetes and food preparation. Many of those who live in Nogales and Hermosillo come from far away and conditions very different from the urban center, so they lack understanding of how to live in such conditions. Once Dr. Jorge Pazos moved to Hermosillo from Tijuana, the health programs strengthened in Hermosillo, Caborca and Nogales. As with other ministries, Compañeros sought to train Health Promoters to hold classes in the homes of people in the community.

Eventually, Dr. Pazos also became a pastor, founding the Voz del Desierto Church in Hermosillo, which led to stronger congregations and then was appointed to be the Mexican Co-coordinator of Compañeros. While the U.S. Coordinators have changed, Compañeros has had the fortune of Mission Co-Workers paid by the PCUSA mission agency and who have served more consistently. The consistent leadership of Dr. Pazos has enabled easier transitions between U.S. Coordinators and at least until the departure of David and Susan Thomas, there was a consistent contact with U.S. supporting churches. Since their departure in 2007, that contact has been maintained only by the board and the regular e-newsletter.

The terrorist attacks of 9/11 and the economic collapse of 2008 have both affected Compañeros as it has PBM in general. CeM had another serious disaster in 2007 in the form of Hurricane Henriette that devastated Sonora from Guaymas to Nogales as it did much of southern Arizona. The ensuing difficulties made it more difficult for delegations to come, and disaster assistance became the focus until the area was once more safe for the typical mission delegation. The energy never quite returned. Still, there is much to celebrate. The church in Hermosillo, now under the leadership of the Rev. Ramón García is growing and in process of adding a second story on the church building to expand the ministry. His background in ministries connected to PBM is extensive and his work in building a church from the ground up is making the work in Hermosillo prosper.

For a number of reasons, the community center in Hermosillo had to be closed, the primary reason being that the neighborhood grew too dangerous. However, the church, located in a middle class area, has sought to continue the work on a smaller level out of its doors. Mission delegations continue to come from Wisconsin and other places to do Bible Schools with the children and provide dental and health clinics.

For Rev. García and his church the relationships with the delegations from the U.S. are an important blessing in their lives. As the pastor says, "Our spirituality is a bit different than it would be without the mission delegations from the U.S. We believe that it is a gift to experience our brothers and sisters who come from the U.S., laying aside their comfort to come so far to suffer discomfort to be in ministry with us. We realize it as a blessing that builds us spiritually. Their capacity to share in a spirit of unity is a very beautiful thing. It is a special faith."

The church Dr. Pazos leads in Nogales is doing well. Another church is being started with the aid of the Presbyterian Church of America but falters under the same issues that plague all the work: leadership quality, placement within the community, and goals of the parties. The board of Compañeros includes one member from the PCA, what to many members of the PCUSA seems odd, has been developing along the border for several years as the PCA develops interest in ministry in México. However, as Dave Thomas, former co-coordinator of CeM and then regional liaison for México of World Mission said, "With regard to theology and biblical understanding the Mexican church is much more comfortable with the PCA, yet, along the border where the pastors have known the PCUSA for many years, there is considerable trust and desire to continue working with the PCUSA."

Susan and David Thomas were called to work in Latin America in the early 1990s. They applied to the PCUSA World Mission for whatever work they may be able to do asking to be sent to Latin America. Never in their wildest dreams did they ever expect to be sent to the border, nor did they desire such an appointment, but in 1999 the call came, they went to language school, and began work in September, 2001. They decided it had to be God's will for them to go there but early on found the work daunting. CeM had work in six cities two of which, Nogales and Hermosillo, were quite large. At first, they asked, "Why us? and Why here?" but they came to believe they had actually been called to this place and persevered and believed they were able to do good work. By the time they arrived one of the biggest challenges had been addressed, namely, Dr. Pazos, who had lived in Hermosillo several hours south of Nogales had moved to Nogales making the working relationship between the co-coordinators more effective.

The team saw a need to lead more intentionally the Mexican pastors and the mission delegations to greater cross-cultural awareness. They saw four problems with mission delegations, somewhat addressed earlier.

1. Some mission delegations were all male. They came to build stuff, which they did and for good, but they never got engaged with the people. They built, grabbed lunch at a fast food and dinner at a nice restaurant, never engaging with the Mexican community.

2. Even the delegations with both men and women tended to simply operate as if they were at home. Men doing men's stuff and women women's stuff. They stayed in a place apart from the people and interacted only marginally with the Mexicans.

3. When delegations did interact, they tended to be soft hearted towards those they interacted with and giving money or promising to send or bring some special item of need on return to specific persons without regard to the affect such generosity had on the church and community.

4. The Mexicans seldom participated in the work of the delegations.

Dr. Pazos and the Thomases worked together to do more cultural education. At first delegations resisted. One delegation only included men until Mr. Thomas encouraged them to include women in the delegation. The result was a very different kind of experience and interaction with the communities.

Cultural education came in both subtle and explicit education. Explicit education was formal and didactic, teaching groups through talks with professionals and program leaders about the reasons for the situation in the border regions addressed above and below. The groups began to visit the Border Patrol to hear its own testimony about what it was doing and why, an experience that had at least three responses: total support for their work, total aversion, and those who found the issue somewhat overwhelming.

Most importantly, they worked to have the delegations engage with the Mexican people and vice versa. Instead of the delegations working and going to restaurants, they had the delegations eat the evening meal at the homes of the church people. That required that the delegations and the Mexican people work together gathering tables and chairs from the church and transporting them and then setting them up at the home, often in the street. Needless to say, the street scene gained the attention of the community, an opportunity to share the faith and to expose the community to the U.S. Presbyterians who came to learn and serve. As time passed the delegation members and the people in the churches with which they worked began to form deep relationships. Delegations came to understand why mission tourism serves only U.S. curiosity not the people on the mission fields. Both the Mexican and the U.S. people came to love each other.

Sometimes that love took directions that were problematic. Delegation members would get attached to individuals in the church and want to do something for that person. David told of a U.S. delegation member who asked a woman who was a seamstress if she needed anything to make her work easier or better. The woman replied that she really needed a sewing machine. With heart in the right place but not understanding the context, the delegation member went home, collected contributions and the next year returned to México with a sewing machine for her Mexican friend. The delegation member asked when she could present the machine to her friend. Mr. Thomas asked her if she wanted to do this publicly. She responded yes. One of the hardest things for U.S. coordinators to do is tell people the truth when they know it will hurt. He tried as best he could to share with her that it would be all right if she made such a presentation in public to the whole church that would then make the sewing machine available to all the women, all of whom needed such a gift. Also, he shared that if the one woman got such a valuable gift, several months wages for a Mexican, then it encouraged them to cozy up to individuals in the delegation in hopes of getting such largesse. The final problem is that the woman who received the gift would receive the envy and jealousy of the others in the church. Fortunately, the delegation member understood.

The problems were not one way. Mexicans are almost universally quite poor in comparison to their U.S. counterparts. The pastors and their families are in as much need as most of their parishioners. Since the pastors are in a better position than most to grow close to the delegation members, they have opportunities to make requests of the delegations and the delegations often responded with kind heartedness. The education had to go both ways, teaching the pastors that what they were doing was unfair to their churches and to delegations. For example, making requests for the whole community for school scholarships was appropriate but to request them only for their children was not. The possibilities for such abuse were manifold.

However, as time passed there was growth both among the U.S. delegations and churches and among the Mexicans. As in every place I visited and every U.S. participant I interviewed, the one thing they valued most was the deep sense of Christian community they enjoyed and growing to see the other as being like them. The Thomases shared the story of a time after a dinner in a home when a delegation member asked the hostess, "Do you wish to come to the U.S.?" She responded that she did not. "I see the U.S. on TV and I have always thought it a dangerous place where everyone carries guns to shoot people. They are mean and violent people in the U.S. so I do not wish to go there. They also say they do not want me there." Then with tears in her eyes, she said, "Now I know that there are Americans who are not like that because I have gotten to know you and love you. I know you love and serve Jesus as I do. I thank God that now I know all Americans are not like on TV. It makes me feel better, but I like it here where I live. I don't need to go to the U.S."

PART III: The Border Today: Prospects and Challenges

If one had visited the U.S./México Border in 1980 and not returned until 2012, one would be surprised by how much things have changed and how much has stayed the same. The most obvious changes are in infrastructure: border crossings, fences, roads, schools, and the like. There is apparent economic development, but the disparity between the north side and the south side of the border is still poignant. What lies below the surface in the shadows of the border is the most disturbing change.

Chapter 1: Transitions

Porous Borders to Militarized Zones

Shirley Jewell, a founding member of Frontera de Cristo in 1984, still serves on the board. She has lived in Douglas, AZ since the 1960s. She testifies that when she and her husband first moved to Douglas, there was no sign of a border with the exception of the monuments set by surveyors to indicate where the border was. "If you wanted to go to México, you just walked across. No documents required. Same for the Mexicans. We went to Agua Prieta to buy our vegetables and fruit which were very good. We can't do that anymore. That's hurt them a lot." Other long term residents on both sides recall those days.

From 1980 to the middle of the 1990s little change took place in regard to border enforcement. Most unauthorized entries took place in clandestine ways, but the types were varied. In 1992, while waiting to cross from México to the U.S. at the port of entry, I watched children, teenagers and adults waiting to cross at holes in the chain link fences that demarcated the border. They were waiting until the sparsely deployed Border Patrol, called 'La Migra', moved on. Then with considerable agility, they crawled through and ran to cover in the U.S. Later in the day I was as likely to see a Border Patrol van come to the U.S./Mexican port of entry to drop a van load of boys and girls off and watch them to be sure they walked back to México. Most often these adolescent offenders had bags from Radio Shack, WalMart, J.C. Penney and other merchants in their hands. Some had crossed to see grandparents, aunts, uncles, cousins, or friends who live in the U.S. That kind of activity was obviously not very clandestine and fairly simple, and as regards the young people, everyone looked on it with a bit of humor.

Others though crossed with the hope of not getting picked up and being able to make it to the interior of the U.S. to find a job, visit family, join family already in the U.S., and, in some but very few cases, to carry out criminal activity. These more clandestine crossings took place in many cases in the same sort of way as those mentioned above, but usually in areas where detection was less likely. They went to the outskirts of the towns and cities, crossed in the middle of the night, and often used tunnels and drainage pipes to make their crossing. In the 1980s television networks showed videos of the frightening scenes of immigrants jumping the fences between Tijuana and San Diego and then running with their bags and children across the busy freeways in hopes they could find safety and cover before the Border Patrol found them.

Those were simpler days. Fences were poorly maintained chain link. Even the fences in the most densely populated areas of Tijuana, Nogales, Juárez, and Matamoros were not big deterrents. Like locks on our homes that simply keep honest people honest, the fences only kept the most timid from crossing. Even the most timid people could find the courage to cross with little trouble, and folks did in fairly large numbers. But most were like the children and teenagers whom I watched cross; they went back the same day or, at times, after a longer visit with family.

Drugs were also a part of the problem in the 1990s. Moving people was lucrative, but not as lucrative as drugs, so drug traffickers paid 'mules' to transport drugs. In those days they did not have to be very creative because detection equipment was archaic. Enforcement depended on drug sniffing dogs whose noble efforts were less than satisfactory. Dogs suffer from stress just as humans do and eventually had to be replaced. They also had a fairly low success rate at detecting drugs, so control was seriously unreliable. Sometimes young people are paid to cross a backpack of marijuana or brick of cocaine, but most often the dealers hid the drugs out of sight in vehicles and paid the driver to deliver the drugs. Traffickers did not worry about detection; their losses were considered part of doing business as were the legal fees for bail and lawyers in the U.S. or México, and a bribe here or there. Seldom did the mules or drivers rat them out.

The bottom line was that enforcement was minimal, especially when it came to immigration. In fact, immigration enforcement was somewhat casual. There was far more concern about drugs, but in the 1970s and 1980s more drugs crossed into the U.S. by airlines, boats, and private airplanes than via the highway. While the border with México was porous, the shorelines and border with Canada were open to all. The only thing our shorelines and Canadian border lacked were welcome signs. Clandestine landing strips dotted the landscape in the southern U.S. where small planes could land and deliver drugs and be gone in minutes.

Under pressure from a variety of interests, especially those concerned about drugs and immigration, The Immigration Reform and Control Act of 1986[40] became law with support from President Reagan and congressional members. The bill made knowingly hiring undocumented immigrants illegal. It provided a more extensive guest worker program for agriculture and amnesty for persons who were already in the country without documents, its most controversial aspect. An estimated 3 million persons applied for and received legal residency under the law. The law did not provide undocumented persons automatic access to citizenship. It only permitted them to apply like everybody else.

The employer sanction was ineffective for a number of reasons.

1. It only applied to persons who employed more than three persons. Therefore, wealthy persons

---

[40] This Act and other relevant information is readily available through government and other sources on the internet.

who hired a maid, groundskeeper and nanny were not affected. It was this hole in the law that eventually became a problem for two of President Bill Clinton's first appointments. While they appointees were not breaking the law by hiring an undocumented worker, they were breaking the spirit of the law and, worse, found it to their advantage not to withhold and pay Social Security and income taxes which was a legal infraction no matter whom they employed. These debacles may have led to the I.R.S. revising rules to create the Individual Tax Identification Number in 1996 through which undocumented persons could file and pay their taxes or get refunds if their employer overpaid.

2. At least according to some, providing amnesty sent the wrong signal to would be undocumented immigrants. Some critics of the legislation claim it opened the flood gates, a clear example of false cause. However, it did give the impression that the U.S. may very well offer amnesty on a regular basis. What affect the law had on new immigration is hard to determine and most believe it was little because the flood of undocumented immigrants did not start until many years later. The recent immigrants are mostly seeking a better economic future for their families despite the risk.

3. The guest worker program quickly proved to be inadequate to meet the needs of U.S. agriculture in a growing economy with low domestic

unemployment, a factor that persisted in the U.S. from the end of the recession of 1981-82 until 2008. The result was that foreign men and women who were willing to take low paying jobs were enticed to come to the U.S. to work in jobs that paid in a day what they could only hope to make in a week or a month at home. Many men and women who came under the guest worker program disappeared into the landscape once the work was done thus overstaying their visa. Visa overstays remain a large segment of our undocumented population and such persons come from every corner of the globe, not just from Latin America.

In 1990 under pressure from business and industry, the congress passed the Immigration Act of 1990 which increased the total number of visas in all categories to an aggregate 700,000 per year. It provided temporary protective status to some immigrant populations from nations in turmoil from political strife or natural disaster, and created a number of business related visa categories. The most controversial portion was a repeal of English language proficiency requirements thus igniting the "English Only" movement.

By the time President Clinton took office there was a clamor for doing something about undocumented immigrants. Most of the clamor was focused on our southern border, despite that Latin Americans made up only part of the problem. The southern border was the easiest place for congress and an embattled president to showcase that they took this problem seriously. So on October 1, 1994 the experiment called "Gate Keeper" was launched by the Border Patrol with great fanfare. This operation followed on a less ambitious operation in El Paso, TX the year before.

Percentage Rise in Various Categories

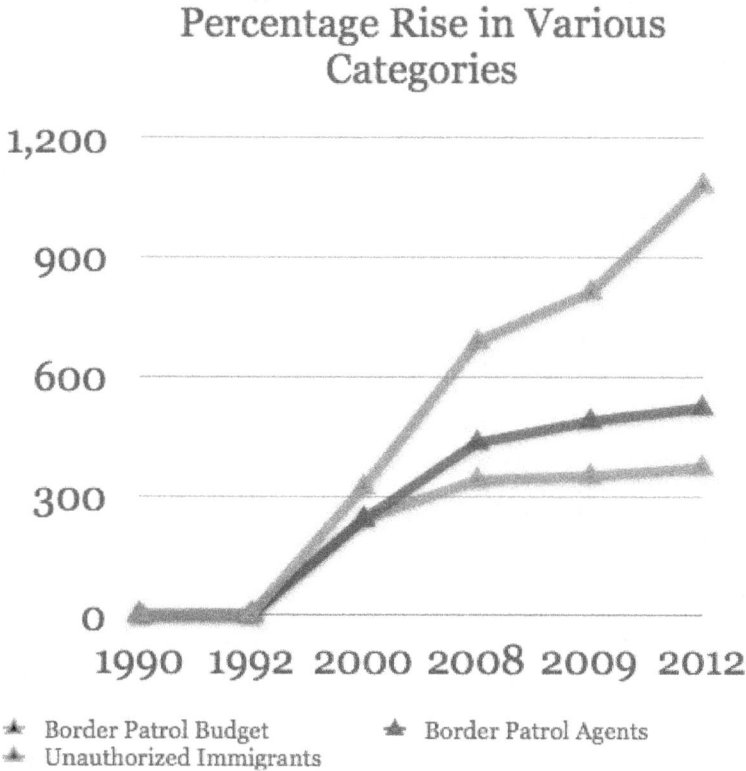

Data collected from website of U.S. Customs and Border Protection and Pew Charitable Trust.

The operations simply deployed many more Border Patrol agents along the border resulting in a tremendous reduction of daytime attempts at crossing and a 70percent reduction in apprehensions in the El Paso area.

Having already spent millions erecting more fences of surplus portable landing strip tarmac from Vietnam[41], attorney general Janet Reno decided to implement further efforts in San Diego where nearly forty percent of all unauthorized entries took place. The operation concentrated efforts on the western most fourteen miles of the border around the Imperial Beach crossing. Needless to say the operation worked to some extent, reducing crossings in that stretch and forcing crossers into the more rugged and less hospitable regions where they were less likely to cross. Still, the plan only worked in part. Evidence suggests that the number of crossers stayed the same; they just went elsewhere.

As time passed the strategy was extended. With the passage of the Illegal Immigration Reform and Immigrant Responsibility Act of 1996 and other budgetary adjustments the budget for the Immigration and Naturalization Service doubled from that of 1993 and the number of Border Patrol agents also doubled. Fences were re-enforced or were being re-enforced or installed in all of the metropolitan areas along the border. The results were dramatic—apprehensions did rise but no evidence proves a decrease in unauthorized entries. Until the 2008 recession, border crossings seemed to increase in proportion to the increase in budgets and personnel. (See chart below.) The problem is that we can only guess at the actual number of unauthorized crossings.

---

[41] There are reliable people who give a different war. The first of these walls predate even the Gulf War under President George H.W. Bush. Later walls could have been constructed from similar materials from the later wars.

Despite the difficulties and dangers of crossing, unauthorized immigrants from Latin America do return home for various weddings, funerals, the quinceañera of daughters, and just to reconnect with

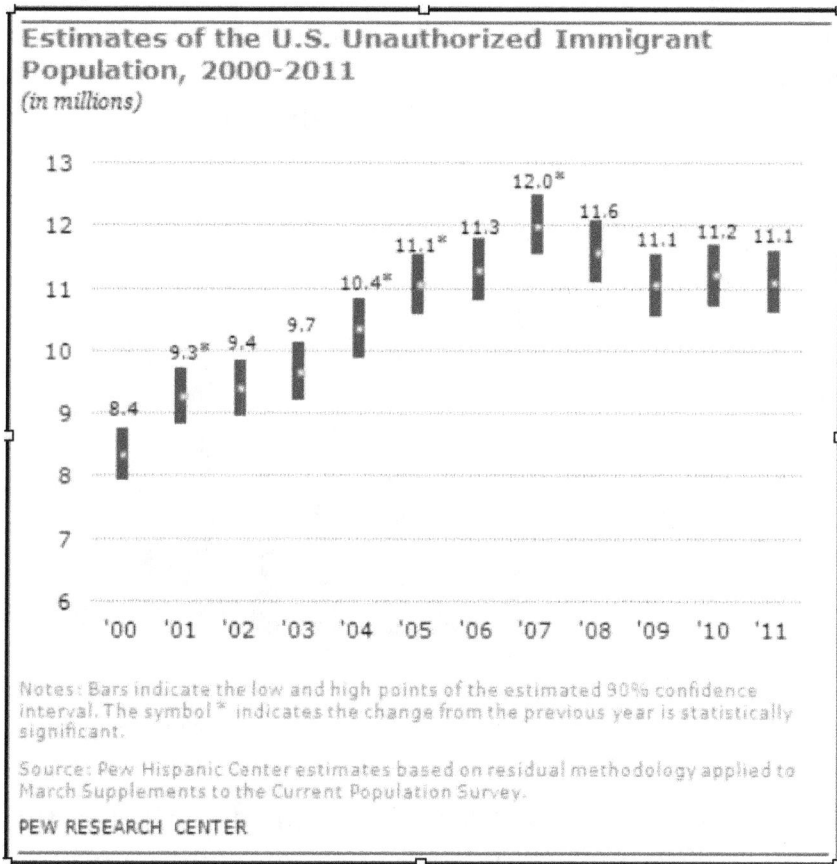

Estimates of the U.S. Unauthorized Immigrant Population, 2000-2011
(in millions)

13

12.0*

12   11.6
                    11.3
             11.1*   11.1   11.2 11.1

11   10.4*

         9.7

10   9.3* 9.4

9   8.4

8

7

6

   '00 '01 '02 '03 '04 '05 '06 '07 '08 '09 '10 '11

Notes: Bars indicate the low and high points of the estimated 90% confidence interval. The symbol * indicates the change from the previous year is statistically significant.

Source: Pew Hispanic Center estimates based on residual methodology applied to March Supplements to the Current Population Survey.

PEW RESEARCH CENTER

families. Then, after a brief visit they returned to their U.S. jobs, homes and families by crossing once more without documents.

In 1980 such returns would have been a matter of course. Many from México migrated annually for work on farms, ranches, golf courses, lawn care, pool maintenance, construction and so on. Once the season was over, they returned home. Nobody paid much attention. Returning home now is not only illegal but extremely dangerous. As the security has grown, so have the number of deaths in the deserts. The graph shows what has happened over the years as border security increased.

Older women have told me that they and their

Migrant Deaths in Arizona
(Coalición de Derechos Humanos database)

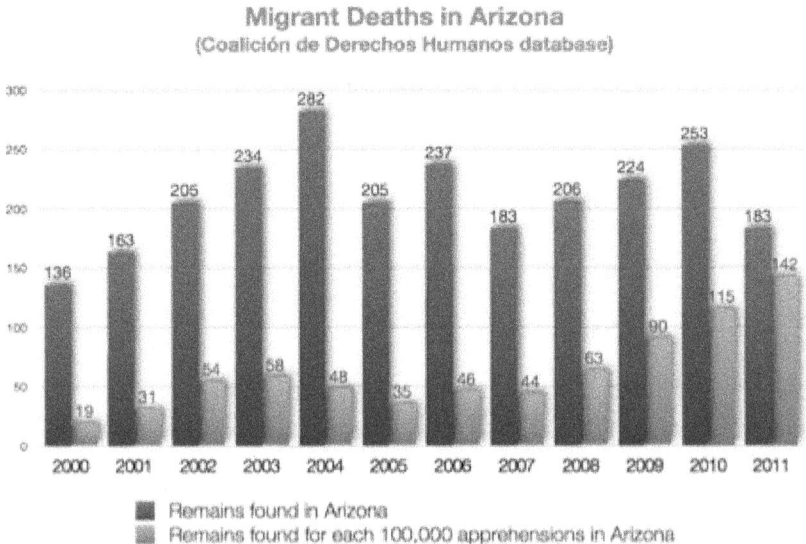

Remains found in Arizona
Remains found for each 100,000 apprehensions in Arizona

husbands once crossed for work year after year in the 1960s, 1970s and 1980s, and now their children protest when they beg the children not to do likewise saying, "Well, you did it all the time when we were kids. Why shouldn't we?" Estela Mora, now a hairdresser in Agua Prieta, lamented, "They do not understand that when we crossed it was not dangerous. We walked right across the border into the U.S., into Douglas, and the rancher picked us up. There were no criminals and we did not have to go way out in the dessert to cross. We went to Colorado to work for the summer and then he brought us back. They treated us well. It's not safe to go anymore. So sad, we had a good life."

Today, over 800 miles of border is fenced with high strength steel structures, surplus portable landing strip tarmac (also made of steel), with stadium lighting illuminating the fence at night, sound and vibration sensors, video cameras, aerial drones, airplanes and helicopters, and a road built for Border Patrol vehicles. The chart shows the increase in Border Patrol agents. Under President George W. Bush, the number of agents doubled and the budget nearly tripled. In summer of 2013, Congress passed a new immigration reform act—Border Security, Economic Opportunity, and Immigration Modernization Act— which will double the number of agents in the Border Patrol, add 800 miles to the fence, shore up portions of the existing fence, and add billions of dollars of technological surveillance.

Department of Homeland Security was initiated and it created Immigration and Customs Enforcement (ICE) by combining the duties of customs with some immigration duties from the former INS. Border Patrol has some jurisdiction on the interior of the U.S., but workplace raids are carried out by ICE. Under President Bush the focus was on suspected terrorists, and job place raids were sporadically carried out. These raids are often brutal invasions that include agents in body armor, masks, and weapons confronting owners, operators and workers who are unarmed. In its first term, the Obama administration carried out hundreds of raids and deported more unauthorized immigrants than President Bush did in eight years. (To date two million).

The Border Patrol is likened to a police force. In fact, much that it does is patrol and watch. Most of the agents became agents because the pay is good, the benefits are better and, if the past predicts the future, the future looks good for advancement. The best part is that while the job is dangerous at times, it is less dangerous than a lot of police work in cities.

The down sides are:

1. Where one has to live and work. With few exceptions the border communities in the U.S. are not destination resorts.

2. The work is stressful, and the agents often remark that they are called on to do things they'd prefer not to do. More than one agent has told me that his or her Christian faith tells him or her one thing, yet the job demands another.

3. The agents often come on horrifying scenes of human misery: women and children having died in birthing; men and women who have died of dehydration which can result in horrific physical trauma; children sitting beside parents who are dying or have expired; being called to the scene of rape and murder perpetrated most often by drug and human traffickers; and, of course, decomposing bodies or skeletal remains.

The agents all know that most of those they apprehend want the same thing they want—to feed their families and gain a better life, yet, Border Patrol agents go out with the most sophisticated military equipment: pistols, automatic rifles and other weapons; night vision goggles, high powered binoculars and video telescopes; communications gear developed for the military; helicopters, airplanes, and drones that watch the border; and now satellite real time images. One wonders how anybody successfully crosses the border without being apprehended.

Just the number of agents seems enough. Presently there are ten agents for each mile of border. Under the proposed legislation, there will be enough personnel to post an agent every thousand feet twenty-four hours per day. Evidently, not all agents are deployed watching and apprehending. Some are administrators, others work in transporting those who are apprehended, some work in stations monitoring the surveillance screens. However, with modern equipment more and more are in the field.

If fences, lighting, sensors, video surveillance and the like were not enough, a factor that contributes even more to the feeling that the border is in lock down is that agents are now deployed as in prisons in fixed locations where they can be seen. In dense areas each team surveils a small area; in rural areas they may watch a large swath of the border. They move from their locations only on command or permission. They often apprehend, but their first responsibility is to see and report. Should the crossers move through their lines, a second line of mobile agents seeks and apprehends. If the second line fails to intercept, it informs a third line of defense. Today, the deserts of the southwest crawl with agents.

While apprehension of unauthorized immigrants is a part of the story carried out by the Border Patrol and ICE, the final aspect of the militarization of the border is the detention centers, a soft name for a not so soft reality. One would expect that such centers are located only along the border, are owned by the federal government, and are required to treat their residents with respect and humanity. All are incorrect.

The facilities are spread across the nation.[42] While Texas and California have the most such facilities, they are also found in unlikely places far from the border and in places where one suspects there are few unauthorized immigrants. Yet, because immigrants live in nearly every part of our nation, unauthorized immigrants do also and ICE uses a vast array of facilities as it reports: "ICE currently uses more than 300 local and state facilities operating under intergovernmental service agreements; seven contract detention facilities and eight ICE-owned facilities. Approximately sixty-seven percent of the ICE population is in a local or state facility, seventeen percent in contract detention facilities, thirteen percent in ICE-owned facilities, service processing centers and three percent in other facilities such as Bureau of Prison (BOP) facilities, which are funded either through congressional appropriations to BOP or through ICE reimbursement." When apprehended, the person is shipped to the most convenient facility or the one with space. Some facilities are for men, others for women, and some for women with children. Men

---

[42] http://www.ice.gov/detention-facilities/index.htm

will be separated from wife and child but regardless are seldom housed in a family facility where women with their children are detained. Unaccompanied juveniles and children are turned over to Department of Health and Human Services Office of Refugee Resettlement for placement in appropriate places.[43]

Where do the unaccompanied minors come from? Many of the children cross to re-unite with parents, grandparents, aunts, uncles, siblings. Many are also victims of human trafficking, especially girls. Others are the result of ICE raids that apprehend parents and leave their children abandoned. For the most part children receive equivalent care as do domestic children, but juvenile facilities and foster care have a checkered history.

Persons had an average stay in the detention centers of 30.49 days in FY 2008. That is time for processing, adjudication in court, and disposition of the deportation if so ordered. However, the literature is filled with stories of: show trials and abuse; lack of appropriate food and water, medical care, medications for chronic diseases; extreme cold or heat; unclean bedding; sexual abuse; and actual physical abuse when detainees complain. DHS has created standards for the centers, but case files mount of the abuse of such standards by officers.

Unfortunately, family detention centers, both operated by private prison corporations, have been the center of controversy resulting from policies that did not take into account that they were housing children

---

[43] Ibid.

whose needs were quite different from adults and who react in dramatically different ways to the prison environments than adults may. Responding to complaints, the T. Don Hutto Family Detention Center in Williamson County, TX opened its doors to reporters. Lawyers and others who visited the center often on business reported that the facility had been markedly spruced up for the tour. Since reporters are almost never given access to the residents of detention facilities, the only information is that passed on by visitors who are lawyers and religious workers.

When we discover that the Corrections Corporation of America receives $2.8 million per month for operations at Hutto, one wonders why conditions in the center are not pristine. Yet, a for-profit corporation has one mission—to make money. CCA lobbies heavily for immigration and criminal justice legislation that will improve its bottom line as more and more states and the federal government opt for outsourcing many government services to private companies. As many parallels as there are between border enforcement and military exercises, the outsourcing of prisons in the U.S. is not unlike the outsourcing of military facilities and security operations to private corporations in Iraq and Afghanistan, a plan that has resulted in horror stories of abuse.

In Arizona, as early as 2001, State Legislator Russell Pearce began his own crusade to take the state into the fray. Proposal after proposal sought to limit those who entered the U.S. without documents to the dark underside of Arizona life. His actions were a reaction to the incredible transformation of Arizona which had 'experienced a doubling of the Latino population, especially in the Phoenix area. Having served in the sheriff's department under the now infamous Joseph M. Arpaio, Pearce had been injured by a Latino in 1997. After beginning his crusade in the legislature, his son was wounded by an undocumented immigrant while he was serving a warrant during a search for a homicide suspect.

Relentlessly, Pearce has pursued anti-immigrant legislation attacking immigrant children by restricting their access to education and other services of the state. He introduced a bill that was as anti-business as it was anti-immigrant by making hiring undocumented workers a crime. The penalty was the suspension of one's business license for six months on first offense and permanent revocation of the license on second offense. Pearce was displeased that the federal government was not enforcing its own law in this regard, so Arizona had to. The law passed despite formidable opposition from the business community of Arizona. The result was that state law enforcement would be deployed against the scourge of immigrants adding to the army of law enforcement already in place.

In Texas in 2005 Governor Rick Perry took another tack and by executive decision initiated Operation Line Backer increasing local law enforcement along the border with the purpose of apprehending undocumented immigrants. Several years later, when Republican legislators introduced a barrage of anti-immigrant legislation like that passed in Arizona, the

Latino Caucus reached out to business leaders and co-opted pro-business Republicans to counter the legislation. Business took the position that it was impossible to do business in Texas without the undocumented labor force and that Texas and the U.S. sorely needed legislation that would provide a safe haven for undocumented workers to become legalized. The alliance succeeded and no new legislation was passed, but the law enforcement on the border remained in place further increasing the sense that the border was in lock down mode.[44]

Family businesses to organized crime

Until 1924 there was almost no border surveillance. During the revolution in México, U.S. Army troops were sent to the southwest border to watch for Pancho Villa, but there was no concern about immigration. The U.S. was helping its friend, President Porfirio Dias, in his war against the "communists".

With the National Origins Act of 1924, the southern border began to attract attention. The act did not exclude Mexican and South Americans but did exclude Asians under its affirmation of the 1882 Chinese Exclusions provisions. Since the Asians entered through México, a regularized patrol of the border regions began. The plan remained mostly a formal idea of few substantial results because the region was vast and open. Prohibition of alcoholic beverages in the U.S. (1920-1933) added to the work of the Border Patrol

---

[44] Information concerning Arizona and Texas is drawn from Jeffrey Kaye, Moving Millions, Chs. 10-11.

charging it with intercepting alcohol smuggled from México.

In the 1930s the Great Depression placed pressures on immigrant populations. Calls went out to remove foreigners. The federal government responded by rounding up large numbers of persons, many of whom were citizens of the U.S. and whose families went back centuries before the Spanish explorers. Estimates are that 500,000 persons were deported without regard to family unity or citizen status.

The introduction of the Bracero Plan in 1942, which sought contracts with México to obtain labor to fill gaps left by the deployment of most U.S. men to World War II, opened the doors to the south. While most of the migrant labor brought north for that project was sent home, many found ways to stay in the U.S. This plan was not revoked until President Lyndon Johnson led its revocation under pressure from labor unions which considered it exploitative. Under the plan laborers from México were bound to the farmer or factory owner for whom they worked. If the workers left their position, they had to return to México. The conditions under which they were forced to work and live were of little concern to the employers or the government. Little attention was given this state of affairs until Edward R. Murrow raised it dramatically in his documentary "Harvest of Shame" in 1960.

In 1965 the Immigration and Nationality Act lifted restrictions based primarily on nationality but for the first time restricted legal immigration from México. Up to this time Mexicans only had to prove they were citizens of México to enter the U.S. and laws only prohibited working without permits. The act had little bite.

For the first time, crossing the border was illegal unless one did so through a port of entry and had properly been admitted. If one did otherwise, the entry was considered unauthorized. Still, enforcement was poor and little attention was paid. However, immigration began to accelerate from the south as proxy wars began to flair in Latin America.

Already, Cuba had fallen to communism and Florida was flooded with Cuban immigrants who met with the enmity of the Anglo population. In the late 1960s into the 1980s immigrants from the south flowed north to escape the wars of Central America. Despite its having been an unstable region for much of the post-colonial period, the Central American nations and many South American nations took on disturbing Communist leanings. The U.S. became engaged in trying to shore up ally governments many of which were tyrannical. While the amount of actual aid to the rebel forces from the Soviet Union, China, and Cuba was overstated at the time, the three communist nations seeking influence were raising concerns among the staunch anti-Communists in the U.S.

The proxy wars in Latin America were horribly oppressive and dangerous so thousands of Central Americans fled north to escape political oppression and economic basket cases. They entered the U.S. without documentation and were unwelcome reminders of U.S. support of tyranny and oppression. In fact, the U.S. was being flooded by refugees from proxy wars around the world. Most refugees were fleeing governments which were unfriendly to the U.S.—Vietnam, Cambodia, Laos. Despite which nation was sending, the perception was that millions of refugees were descending on a stressed and, consequently, inhospitable U.S.

By the mid 1980s there were several million persons living in the U.S. who had not been granted any kind of legal status. Many were economic refugees, especially those from the Caribbean and Central America. The wars and political instability had led to economic instability and people came to the U.S. to work and send money home. While many proxy war refugees received political refugee status, they were viewed by the traditional populations as aliens who were sucking up national resources which could be better deployed for Americans.

The development of the Free Trade Zone in México, the building of hundreds of factories and the resulting increase of population made the border a far more fluid area. Passage across the border was easy enough and the 'coyote' business was growing by leaps and bounds. Already in most areas the enterprises some refer to as "coyotes" and others as tour guides were in business. In the 1980s and 1990s men and women were employed to help persons unfamiliar with the border region cross into the U.S. and connect with persons in the U.S. who could help them get to their destination, or, at times, help them with job placement. The whole operation was quite informal, there were few real criminals involved, and most of the clients either knew the coyote or had been referred to them by friends or relatives. The coyotes most often had friends or relatives in the sending community.

The costs were minimal. Depending on where along the border the crossing would occur and the services required once in the U.S., the costs were from $80 to as much as a couple hundred dollars. While drugs were a part of border life, they were being trafficked by drug rings that were not connected with coyotes or the vast majority of migrants. Since it was illegal to cross except at official entry points, guides were needed to show one where to cross safely, but illegally.

By the time Ronald Reagan became president in 1980, California had gone through some torturous immigration debates. It was especially hard hit by refugee migration from the Pacific rim, México and Central America. Tijuana, México had been a huge metropolis for a very long time whose Mexican residents flooded in and out of California and with them many Central Americans.

President Reagan and the congress worked to pass an act that would deal with the question of the undocumented population and seek a solution to slow future immigration of undocumented persons. After fits and failures, the Immigration and Control Act was passed. As stated above, the act imposed employer sanctions for the first time, provided an amnesty program that gave persons a process to obtain legal residency documents, and to enter the process for citizenship. The amnesty was restricted to persons who worked in certain agricultural enterprises and to persons who entered the U.S. before January 1, 1982 and had lived continuously in the U.S. since then.

President Reagan was personally inclined toward immigrants because he believed that anyone who wanted to come to the U.S. and become a part of its culture should be welcomed. However, he had run up against anti-immigrant forces as governor of California so when he approached the issue as president, he did so with greater caution and assurances of a better watch on the southern border.

Still little changed on the border from 1984 until 1996–crossing the border required fairly easy to obtain documents or some creativity. Throughout the 1980s and 1990s once the immigrants entered the U.S., they could catch a bus or even a flight to the destination. After the terrorist attacks of September 11, 2001, airport security grew and air travel became impossible or quite costly because fake driver's licenses or IDs had to be bought for such travel. As time passed after 9/11, bus travel was even precarious because buses did nothing to avoid check points, so transportation vans and autos had to be provided by the coyote enterprise for travel to other parts of the U.S. which increased the cost.

As crossers were forced to cross farther and farther into the dessert, the costs increased all the more. Coyotes had to provide a guide and transportation to the border crossing. The guide continued with the group into the U.S. and to the connection with the transportation persons. This factor meant the guide was in jeopardy of being caught, so the coyote enterprise had to provide legal assistance and other "protections". Protection took several forms: bribes of Border Patrol, immigration and customs officials in the U.S., and lawyers in the U.S. were kept on retainers to deal with the guides or the transportation people if they were apprehended.

There were other dangers. Clients often died. The desert is a dangerous place to be. Dehydration kills and does so quickly. Migrants cannot carry enough water to properly hydrate. Nor can they carry enough food. The trek can be as much as seventy miles or five to seven days. If you falter, you get left. If you get sick, nobody carries you. Dangerous animals are present everywhere even if you cannot see them—snakes, scorpions, venomous spiders, mountain lions, coyotes, and javelina.

Getting across is difficult and extremely dangerous. Using the desert for cover makes the trip more so. I have friends who have taken the trips of migrants to experience what the migrants experience in some measure. The difference is that a supply and first aid van or truck accompanied my friends with water, food and medical supplies. Many drop out because it is simply too arduous. Some have been evacuated by helicopter from the desert due to illness induced by the desert conditions. The undocumented crossers lack that kind of support. They are at the mercy of the environment.

Increased security and surveillance required the transport systems to find houses in which to hide immigrants until they could be transported to their destination. Since a house could only be used until the network discovered it was being watched or had been raided, someone had to be constantly looking for new properties. Rents are high and protection requires increased personnel.

As border enforcement grew stronger, fences extended farther; difficulty and dangers of crossing increased; meeting up with transportation in the U.S. became more precarious; safe houses were needed; and the need for transportation for transporting persons from the safe houses to wherever the persons wished to go in the U.S. increased. The result of all this was increased cost. Having a mature travel infrastructure made the system more easily detectable so more bribes had to be paid.

All the above may be boiled down to three factors that led to major change. First, the complexity of the business became too difficult and beyond the pale of what friends and family might do. Second, the money was now worth the effort for criminals. Third, criminals already had networks on the U.S. side and the necessary connections in México. Enter organized crime.

Organized crime was already paying bribes to law enforcement in México and in the U.S. for protection for the drug trade, so it made sense that it would edge out the mom and pop coyotes and take over when the money became good enough in the business of moving humans. Since the U.S. was becoming more effective at finding drugs hidden in vehicles, the drug rings needed other ways to cross the drugs. The guides and migrants were excellent "mules" (persons used to transport drugs). The migrant was often given a break on her or his travel plan if she or he agreed to carry drugs. Guides were paid more for doing so. Drug and human trafficking became a symbiotic arrangement. However, with the changes, the majority of drugs still pass through ports of entry or enter by air or sea.

Organized crime and extreme violence

The results have been traumatic. While the border towns were centers of drug trafficking for years, México was not the first place one thought about in that regard until the new millennium. We still think more of Colombia than México, yet, México is becoming the new Colombia not because of farming the drugs, which does happen in México, but because it is a major avenue for drugs to travel to the U.S. from other countries and the violence is growing in intensity. The same issues the U.S. dealt with during the 1980s in Colombia, namely, the large cartels, became the issue in México.

There is a difference. In Colombia human trafficking was not an aspect. In México human trafficking is growing at an astonishing rate. There are numerous reports of migrants being held in near slavery, sold into sexual slavery, or forced into prostitution.[45] Often a migrant girl will cross carrying drugs and find herself shipped to some place to become a sex slave or a prostitute and disappearing. Families are unable to do much about her disappearance and the U.S. federal and state governments have not engaged on this crime.

So in México we have the convergence of three highly lucrative businesses that are quite attractive to anyone with a criminal bent. Young men become the front men for the coyote business because it pays far better than working at an honest job. Often they are paid on commission, so they work hard at recruiting migrants who wish to cross. Every bus or train is met by a number of such young men. Sometimes contacts have

---

[45] See for example: Anne-Marie O'Connor, "Mexican cartels move into human trafficking", *Washington Post*, July 27, 2011. [http://articles.washingtonpost.com/2011-07-27/world/35267252_1_sexual-exploitation-marisela-morales-cartels] and Arjan Shahani, "Human Trafficking in México", *Americas Quarterly*, June 14 2013. [http://americasquarterly.org/content/human-trafficking-mexico]

already been made and the agent will seek to recruit more persons. The agent, then, takes the migrants to a gathering place that is usually guarded to keep law enforcement away and to keep any of the clients from leaving to go to another 'bureau'. Guns are involved all along the way.

Today, as drugs and people cross the border into the U.S., the Mexican government has grown more and more concerned about guns being transported into México. In God's mercy, the U.S. is cooperating on this point. Most border stations have U.S. agents looking for people transporting guns into México. Sadly, the U.S. seems incapable of passing laws that will assure that guns bought at gun shows will not go to México, therefore, the traffickers have weapons that are far superior to that of law enforcement. The danger to law enforcement is so great that few men or women wish to become police or soldiers in the areas where the violence is greatest.

When I began drafting this chapter (2010), a twenty year old woman, Marisol Valles García, who became the police chief of Práxedis, a small border town Southeast of Ciudad Juárez, where nobody else would take the job, disappeared. Nobody knew where she was. Some feared she was kidnapped, murdered or worse. Happily, word came that she had filed for asylum for herself and her toddler son in the U.S. but sadly, her life is still in jeopardy because the cartels are able to cross the border almost at will. Cartels are able to get false documents or send someone who is not yet identified to get her. Or they may have an agent of theirs who lives and works in the U.S. make the hit on her. So even if she received asylum here, she was not safe. In addition, U.S. law does not provide asylum for persons just because they fear violence. The violence has to be state sanctioned and thus repressive, however, an exception was found that has given her reprieve. Filmmaker Matthew Paul Olmos has produced a documentary based on her life named "So Go the Ghosts of México".

Border Policy Becomes National Debate

Until the 1980s almost nobody talked about border policy and few concerned themselves with immigration policy. However, as time has passed it is hard to find a person who does not hold an opinion on border policy. The question of what to do about the border and immigration across it is not just a matter of debate because for many migrants the border is a part of their lives.

The debate has gone on to the point of frustration for everyone despite their opinion or involvement. Some in the U.S. honestly feel threatened. Ranchers along the border are not of one mind, but most feel pressure from migrants crossing their land and fear that the violence in México will soon follow. Many people, whether correct or not, believe that undocumented immigrants receive free services without paying taxes and cost the states and federal government more than they pay in taxes should they pay taxes which many do. Since the recession, the cry over immigrants taking jobs from U.S. citizens and legal residents has grown.

Congress has been hamstrung on the issue. Congresspersons and senators who once supported legislation for comprehensive immigration reform no longer do because of the outcry from the right and center over giving amnesty to law breakers. The cry goes out: "Make them go to the end of the line!" "Send them home!" "Secure the border!"

During the George W. Bush administration, Arizona Senator John McCain helped write the legislation for comprehensive reform and co-sponsored it with then Senator Ted Kennedy. Fearing losing his senate re-election bid to an opponent, he re-positioned himself and began talking only of enforcement. Having once argued that no enforcement could secure the border without dealing with the problem of not having enough kinds or numbers of visas, he, like many others, began saying we can do nothing about the other issues until the border is locked down. Having once argued that we could not humanely deport all unauthorized immigrants, he began arguing we cannot solve that issue until we secure the border. He only gives grudging support to the present legislation and does so because it provides for overwhelming force along the border. (See above.)

The argument has escalated to the point that more states have decided to take the law into their own hands and are passing laws that many legal scholars believe are unconstitutional. Law enforcement officials cringe at having to police immigration and lack the resources to do so.

Citizens' groups have formed into militias to police the border and the results are frightening. The Border Patrol fears violence breaking out on the U.S. side, placing them in greater danger. Agents of Border Patrol and ICE already are threatened if they cross the border into México even if for civilian reasons. In 2011 two

Border Patrol agents were assassinated gangland style while returning home from official business in México.

These kinds of events only exacerbate an already overheated debate that has lost all reason. Despite the federal government spending billions on re-enforcing the border with over eight hundred miles of strong fencing, building fences and moats inside fences in some places, doubling the size of the Border Patrol, strengthening ICE, carrying out hundreds of work place raids, and so on, many cry out that the federal government is not doing anything.

If there is a solution in sight, one is hard pressed to find it. The twenty-four hour news cycle does not help. No discussion goes unnoticed and representatives and senators cannot speak freely for fear of being the focus of the next news cycle. The lack of a free discussion without the glare of media lights makes the possibility of solving the problem nearly impossible. Any state or national politician knows that the next election may depend on the ideas she or he may entertain despite how one decides to vote. Even negotiating on the issue has seemed off limits to many sides.

Sadly, few persons in our nation have much information on the issues surrounding immigration. Many focus on the southern border and unauthorized entrance to the nation when nearly 40percent of all undocumented persons living in the U.S. are persons who overstayed their visa or entered on a document that permits visits but not stays in the U.S., a document many persons who live on the borders possess.

Following the 2012 election in which President Barack Obama won re-election partly because the

Hispanic populace voted overwhelmingly for him, the tone of conversation has changed in part. Many Republicans believed that if they do not support and pass an immigration reform bill before 2014 elections, they may be the first party to lose midterm elections in a very long time. So once more Senators McCain and Lindsay Graham became active in pressing for a bill. As time passed, the Republican leadership convinced Fox News to get their commentators on board for reform. Oddly, public opinion shifted to strongly supporting immigration reform, the Senate passed the legislation with a bi-partisan majority with only Tea Party associated Senators holding out. As of March, 2014, the bill languishes with little hope of anything happening in present congress.

· · ·

Given the changed circumstances, the challenges to Presbyterian border ministries are greater today than ever and the need to continue the ministry on the border is growing. New migrants arrive in the border communities every day. Some wish to cross into the U.S. Most simply hope to find work. Some come and stay for a while seeking work but become discouraged and cross. Many still die in the attempt.

Each day migrants who have been apprehended in the U.S. are taken to ports of entry and returned to México. The deportations have created new opportunities for ministry but also challenge the capacity of the ministries to cope. For the churches, the return of so many folks to their communities gives them new opportunities for evangelism and ministry, for alcohol and drug programs, for counseling the discouraged and downtrodden. As one PBM volunteer expressed it, "The harvest is growing and ripening, there just aren't enough workers."

Chapter 2: Continuing Legacy of Extreme Poverty and Wealth

Push Factors in Migration

In migration studies, Push Factors are commonly understood to be negative factors in the sending country; in our case that country is México. However, most sending countries exhibit some common characteristics which are:

1. Lack of jobs

I have addressed this issue in other places for the past. As we enter the next decade of border ministry through Presbyterian Border Region Outreach (See chapter 3 below), the economy of México remains in crisis by many measures. The economy by all macro measures is thriving. Following the disastrous economic downturn of 2008, the economy grew at a 4.3 percent rate from 2010 through 2012. However, it has entered a period of stagnation and in 2013 was expected to have grown by only 1.8 percent.

The problem is that despite significant growth, the economy is still way behind making up for the economic decline of the past few decades and, more importantly, in providing jobs with adequate wages for Mexican laborers to escape poverty. Along the border, the factories still pay the same as in 1990 or only about $50 per week. Households still need three wage earners to begin advancing financially.

2. Civil Strife/War/Political and Religious Persecution

Civil and political strife almost always follows bad economic conditions. So it is in México. Today, that strife is exemplified by extreme violence due to organized crime and gangs. In interview after interview I was told that hardly a family can be found without a family member who is connected to the crime cartels or gangs.

During the presidency of Felipe de Jésus Calderon, 2006 to '12, a significant effort was made to respond to U.S. demands to squelch the drug cartels. The result was extreme violence between the military, national police and the cartels. The murder rate soared, intimidation and extortion became a part of daily life. Many business owners moved away from the most violent areas. Those who could migrated to the U.S. side of the border. Others simply closed up shop as did Astrid Gutiérrez Sichler (See above Part II, Pasos de Fe).

In many cases they burn businesses. In Ciudad Juárez I witnessed lumber yards, junk yards, and many buildings that had been burned out because the owners refused to pay the extortion, shuttered the business and in many cases left the city. The strife has created a loss of employment and hopes for the future.

As I write, the violence continues but is now reduced. Agua Prieta, Nogales and Tijuana and the regions around them are quite safe. However, the strife continues at a high but reduced rate in the cities bordering Texas. Those with whom I spoke in every place attribute the decline in violence to truces between the army, national police, and the various cartels. Where those truces have not been negotiated the violence continues. Agua Prieta only has one cartel which watches carefully and does not permit competition to enter the city. The cartels in Nogales have reached a truce with the

INEGI Statistics by Presidential Term		
President	Homicides per Year	Homicides per Day
Salinas (1989-1994)	93,493	43
Zedillo (1995-2000	80,311	36
Fox (2001-2006)	60,162	27
Calderón (2007-2012)	121,683	56

leadership of the army and police to participate in drug trafficking and human transportation (migration assistance). The cartels have agreed between themselves to a division of the city roughly along the boundary of the highway running south (federal highway 15) from the border towards Hermosillo. Similar arrangements seem to exist in Tijuana which is a far larger city that is now relatively safe given its history as a city of crime.

Statistics indicate that murders rose to alarming rates since 2007 (See table INEGI Statistics by Presidential Terms). After the inauguration of President Enrique Peña Nieto (December 1, 2012), both rhetoric and pledges to bring peace indicated a new direction in policy from that of his predecessor. However, there seems to be no change in the rate of intentional homicides. In fact, the number of intentional homicides appears to be growing on track to around 18,500 by the end of 2013.

Sadly, El Instituto Nacional de Estadística y Geografía (INEGI) shows that prior to the administration of President Felipe Caldarón intentional homicide rates declined for ten years. Once he became president and, under pressure from the U.S. he declared war on the drug cartels, the rates doubled. (See table). México reports actual deaths from the drug war at about 60percent of total intentional homicides based on a poorly defined criteria according to James A. Baker III of the Baker Institute for Public Policy, Rice University.[46]

The drug war is considered by nearly all analysts to be the major cause of this increase in intentional homicides. The U.S. is rightly criticized for its failure to

---

[46] James A. Baker, "México's national crime statistics show no significant decline in homicides and disappearances", Houston Chronicle Blog, http://blog.chron.com/bakerblog/2013/10/is-drug-related-violence-in-mexico-on-the-decline/, November 21, 2013. Viewed same day. By comparison the United Nations Office on Drugs and Crime gives the annual rate per 100,000 for México as 23.7, Colombia as 31.4 and the U.S. as 4.7.

address its drug habit at home while casting blame for its problems onto other governments. Many of my interviewees spoke of their feeling that the U.S. needs to address this problem within its borders and wonder what the intentional homicide rate in the U.S. would be if the U.S. pursued the policies it demands of México and Colombia.

In fact, for the U.S. to carry on the surveillance and constant armed movements that México and Colombia do would be politically caustic. In every city visited, armored trucks carrying fully outfitted soldiers patrol the

Executive Secretariat of Public Security of Mexico	
Year	Inentional Homicides
2007	10,253
2008	13,155
2009	16,118
2010	20,681
2011	22,856
2012	21,700

streets. While most of the time residents and visitors are safe because the cartels are only interested in their competitors and their enemies, one may fall victim to a random shoot out. As a caveat, I spent nearly three months in one or the other of the border cities over the last three years and never heard a single weapon fired nor did I ever feel threatened. That did not mean violence was not happening. While in Nuevo Laredo in May, 2012, a particularly horrid massacre of a family took place while I was in the city. Cities are large and often what takes place in one area does not affect another except as news travels.

3. Environmental Problems

While the environment in México is suffering from nearly every possible environmental problem that every other nation suffers, these issues are not a major push factor. México has suffered some major damage from hurricanes as have many nations of North and Central America, however, the consequences have not been anything like the earthquakes of Central America or the near cataclysmic effect of Hurricane Mitch in Guatemala.

Many areas of México still boast a robust organic agriculture. In several of the coffee growing states the small farmers have not resorted to pesticides and herbicides in their farming. That does not mean the nation's agriculture has not been damaged by such use. Mainly, it is small farmers who primarily seek to feed their families that are preserving both traditional and organic methods. Industrial and large farms have succumbed to heavy input of artificial fertilizers, herbicides, pesticides, and genetically modified seeds.

Therefore, the primary push factors are much the same as in the 1980s and 1990s, namely, economic turmoil and political unrest.

Pull Factors in Migration

1. Economic

Those factors that cause people to leave their homes have a mirror factor in the places they chose to go. Most Mexican migrants come to the U.S. in hopes of jobs or safety or both. In large part the poor come for jobs. The rich come for safety from the violence because they can afford to migrate. Sadly, when the richer people of a nation leave, they leave with their investment capacity and with their knowledge of and capacity to do business damaging further the economy of their home country.

The U.S. has both jobs and safety. While most of the jobs open to Mexican migrants are low paying, the average Mexican can make in a week what it takes them a month to earn in México. If they migrate from the farm, their net income is many times higher in a month than they can earn in a year on the farm. Their labor is in high demand in the fields of the U.S. because they work hard, do not complain, are loyal, and live in conditions most citizens will not endure.

For many impoverished migrants, whether from Africa, Asia, or Latin America, subsistence conditions in the U.S. are better than the conditions at home. Not only are they able to earn enough for rent and food, they can send money home to their families and save money. Many save so they can pay taxes so if an opportunity comes they can apply for legal status.[47] Others save to buy a home for their family or in the U.S. Others save to start a business. Immigrants are by and large industrious and frugal.

2. Network Factors

Where migrants go usually depends on their networks, and the networks are vast for nearly every nationality. Most migrants search out family members, village friends, or acquaintances from their regions. The networks were once simply informal systems like any family system, but as time has passed, they have become more formalized because of the greater enforcement.

Now networks consist of rating systems for where persons can live more safely in the shadows, where work is more available and employers tend to ignore employment laws, or the laws can be subverted the easiest. The organized crime networks have the information and provide direction about where best to enter the U.S. if one wishes to get to Florida, where to seek out family or friends, and so on. That information increases the price, but can be invaluable for the migrant.

3. Impact of U.S. Policy on Migration

---

[47] Many in the U.S. believe immigrants do not pay taxes. However, the IRS for years has provided a mechanism for them to do so through Individual Tax Identification Numbers. Sadly, employers often are not aware that such numbers are available. While working as a volunteer for several years as a preparer with the Volunteer Income Tax Assistance program in Washington D.C., I assisted numerous undocumented immigrants with their taxes using ITN's. Many more would pay their taxes were they to know how and if their employers would become informed.

One cannot underestimate the policies of the U.S. as a pull factor for undocumented immigration. That does not mean welfare and other types of public assistance but immigration policy or lack thereof. It has been nearly seventeen years since the last fairly comprehensive immigration act was passed. The one under President Clinton was only barely comprehensive and notoriously emphasized border control over visa reform and providing a regularized system for immigrants to become legalized and then gain citizenship. The purported line for immigrants to gain legal entry is nearly non-existent for those who are desperate. When one's children are starving waiting in a line that will take thirteen or more years is not an option. One does what one has to.

The fact that there is not a smooth system for farm worker visas that makes it possible for farmers to hire migrant labor and then for that labor to come and go with ease, results in what I have called "Unintentional Immigrants". Most undocumented migrants never wanted to come and stay. However, once they come they know how dangerous returning home can be let alone returning for work in the U.S. So migrant labor becomes immigrant labor.

While national debate rises to a high pitch, farmers and businesses have needs for low skilled workers, a near oxymoron in the U.S. where most people acquire at least a minimal skill level in a trade. Farm work and work in certain industries is not palatable to anyone, and U.S. workers simply do not want the jobs to which immigrants readily flock. The availability of these jobs attracts the migrants despite the policy.

Most characterize the U.S. immigration policy as speaking with "forked tongue". On the one hand we say don't come, but like the comedian, we wave with hidden hand and smirk for them to come on and keep on coming. The challenge to border ministry is knowing how to counsel and respond to such a duplicitous system.

Chapter 3: New Challenges to PBM
Keeping the Vision Alive

This chapter is not intended to be an exhaustive catalog of all that ministries of PBM are doing now. Instead, I hope to give a picture of what is being done with examples of responses to various needs.

Denominational Conflict

In 2010 the General Assembly of the PCUSA sent to the presbyteries amendment 10A to the <u>Book of Order.</u> Passage of the amendment would permit congregations to ordain gay or lesbian persons as Deacons or Ruling Elders whether or not they were living in sexually active relationships. The same decision permitted presbyteries to ordain sexually active gay or lesbian persons to be Teaching Elders (ministers). In effect the amendment returned the decision about who was worthy to be ordained almost completely to the presbyteries and congregations leaving the general criteria:

To those called to exercise special functions in the church-deacons, ruling elders, and teaching elders-God gives suitable gifts for their various duties. In addition to possessing the necessary gifts and abilities, those who undertake particular ministries should be persons of strong faith, dedicated discipleship, and love of Jesus Christ as Savior and Lord. Their manner of life should be a demonstration of the Christian gospel in the church and in the world. They must have the approval of God's people and the concurring judgment of a council of the church.

By spring 2011, it was clear that the amendment was approved. As soon as the approval of the necessary number of presbyteries was assured the amendment took effect. The INPM leadership responded predictably. After a dialogue with leadership of the PCUSA voted on August 19, 2011 to break the long term partnership with the PCUSA. They instructed their ministers, presbyteries and Co-coordinators of PBM to cease relationship with any PCUSA church or presbytery that did not vote against Amendment 10A.

PBM ministries were sent into a tailspin of uncertainty. When I took my trip in 2012, the uncertainty was still in place and apprehension about the future of PBM was high. (See below for more on this subject.)

Continuing ministries to migrants from the south

1. Evangelism

As has been stated above, for the INPM, the focus has always been on establishing new congregations in the borderlands of northern México. While the Mexican Presbyterians did not oppose the social ministries and, as I have shown previously, even find the ministries helpful evangelistic tools, there has always been a sense that those ministries demanded far too much of the resources available to PBM that could better be directed towards paying pastors, congregational development and building churches. As Susan Frerichs explained what happened with regard to Proyecto Amistad, "Once the mission delegations stopped coming and contributions grew less and less, we had to make some decisions. We discovered in our review of the work that most of us felt we had not been listening to the concern of our Mexican brothers and sisters. They wanted us focusing on the needs they felt most urgent. So we began asking what those were."

Chris McReynolds, who followed Frerichs, explained, "By the time I arrived, the violence in México was on everyone's mind. Even the U.S. board members were seeing the violence as one of the major, if not the most important, concern. We tried to think of ways to link the concern over violence with the idea of evangelism. It took a while but we recognized the two were closely linked."

After some more reflection, the ministry began to think about how they could use the Bible as a means of not just leading people to Jesus but to lives of non-violence. Rick Lane, a layman and member of First Presbyterian Church of San Antonio, suggested an organization in the U.S. that published biblical materials for children in Spanish that he believed may be useful. The PA Board reviewed the materials and liked what they saw. They introduced the AMO® Program curriculum and developed a plan with the guidance of the publisher and Francelia McReynolds, who works under the Ministry of Education of INPM.

Thus began Club Amistad. Roberto Medina, Mexican Co-Coordinator of Proyecto Amistad, explained the importance of the program and its approach:

> Mexican culture is primarily Roman Catholic which creates a dependency on the church and the priest. Roman Catholic people believe they are helpless without the church because they are sinners who must go to the priest for salvation creating an inferiority complex. In the Presbyterian Church they discover that they are the children of God with value and self-esteem. This is God's world and they can make it better and change the world. They learn that God has a plan for me and I can change my life and I can be better with the help of God. I am dependent on God who loves me and wants me to have a better life and gives me the power to make a difference. So the esteem of people is increased as they are transformed by Christ.

As described above, the children show important signs of the success of the program. While the program focuses on the children, the parents also become engaged and that gives opportunity to evangelize and teach the principles of non-violent parenting. Attending the Childrens' Day celebrations at the churches was a heartening experience because so many parents were there with their children. Clearly, the postures of the women and the men were more caring and kind than are common in the neighborhoods where a macho attitude was strong.

The leadership of Pueblos Hermanos has been and continues to be focused on evangelism and has seen the health ministries as an excellent outreach and opportunity to share the gospel. As the need for the health ministries declines, a greater effort is being made to turn churches into centers for the communities where children can have a good time in a protected safe space. In a nation where violence seems to be on everyone's mind, having a safe place to be is a way of demonstrating that God loves the children and the people and to "welcome the neighbors into the arms of Jesus" as one Mexican elder told me.

With the aid of Baja Presbyterian Missions (BPM), church development is surging ahead for Pueblos Hermanos. In the last decade, PH and the BPM have helped the Presbytery to form and build new churches and to supply pastors thus reaching 2,000 miles south to the tip of the Baja peninsula.

Pasos de Fe is realizing the dream of cross border evangelism through its new ministry at University Presbyterian Church (UPC) in El Paso, TX, where Rev. Filipe Barandiarán leads a Spanish language service on Sunday afternoon after having led his congregation in

Ciudad Juárez. The service at this writing is nearing one year old and has around thirty participants. UPC has developed opportunities for its two English language services to worship with and fellowship with the Spanish language participants building relationships and enriching the experiences of all those who attend UPC.

At Compañeros en Misión evangelism remains the focus of the ministry. To meet social needs without having to commit ministry resources, the ministry has found ways to partner with social programs Hogar de Esperanza y Paz, A.C., (House of Hope and Peace) where Dr. Pazos' daughter, Jeannette Pazos and Gilberto "Tito" Bojorquez, share duties to provide meals for children, after school activities, programs for migrants who are deported into Nogales, and other needs. Partnering is a way for the ministry to extend its reach but focus on the goal of church development and evangelism.

2. Social Cohesion

Each of the ministries mentioned above work to achieve the goal of social cohesion by which I mean building community. Social cohesion is important in any culture because the stronger neighborhood and community bonds are, the safer people feel, the more freedom they enjoy, and the better able they are to raise their family and accomplish larger goals.

It is not hard to see that as Club Amistads teach children how to resolve many of the situations in a peaceful instead of violent way at home and at school, those children are less likely to grow up and join violent gangs for a number of reasons. One important reason is their sense of self. The children I met in the Club Amistad programs were confident, friendly, bright and quickly responded to questions. Most of us have gone into places where those key factors were not exhibited by the children.

The teachers' corps is well trained in the material and in the core principles of AMO and Club Amistad and are able to live by those principles as a witness and to mentor other parents. All of this leads to a healthy number of people who believe that they can make a difference to reduce violence and they take responsibility to do so.

Every ministry makes use of the church property to build relations with the people of the community, even if only by having festivals, Vacation Bible Schools, and other events to which all in the community are welcome. Such events gather many people and the children into a safe environment and build good will between the church and the community and between the many people in the area around the church. Good will transforms into lack of fear and greater trust which inevitably reduces violence. If I trust my neighbor, I do not need to protect myself against him or her. Most churches at minimum use the opportunities to promote Christian values and good health and self-esteem.

One of the reasons social cohesion plays a role is that the border region is a fluid place. The INPM seeks to place churches in new developing areas where most of the residents are new comers. New comers often go and come. Some come and find jobs in the factories or other enterprises. Others in frustration over not being able to find a job start a business selling whatever they can prepare and sell. All too many come to cross into the U.S. and do so if something does not deter them.

All the ministers and border ministry staff tell possible crossers the dangers of doing so and advise against crossing. However, without a stable community of support, the persons are far more likely to cross than not. Why stay somewhere where you feel alone? I have met men who have tried to cross several times within a few months. They are often returned to México with wounds from their travels, due to a violent criminal or animal attack, or something that happened in the detention center. Some have chosen not to try again because they encounter a place like the ecumenical Migrant Resource Center that Frontera de Cristo and other denominational ministries in the U.S. and México fund and staff.

The Migrant Resource Center in Agua Prieta, Sonora, is well located for its work just to the right of the sidewalk that deportees have to walk on to return to México. As stated earlier, the center provides first aid, a phone to call family or friends, sandwiches, water, rehydration kits, clothes and shoes. Those who cross the desert seldom have shoes adequate for the trek because the sand is coarse and difficult to walk in. Even good shoes quickly take a beating. Most deportees return to México traumatized by weeks in detention centers, lack of health care, hungry and often dehydrated. The Resource Center directs them to other agencies in Agua Prieta that can help them with places to sleep, good meals and recuperation from the trauma.

Like the Migrant Resource Center in Agua Prieta, the HEPAC in Nogales provides assistance and counseling to deportees directing them to services in the city. One hope of providing such services is to help integrate the persons into the community on the border or aide them in returning home in the hopes they will not chose to attempt another crossing and perhaps die in the attempt, a result that is all too common.

3. Health

As mentioned above, as time passes, México has been able to strengthen its health care services which has reduced the need to provide for health and dental services. That is not to say that no needs still exist, however, several of the ministries have found focusing on nutrition, infant and child care classes for women, self-esteem classes and the like are things they can do to promote better heath. The ministries can provide the volunteer leadership and transfer that ministry to primarily Mexican church people. Only Pueblos Hermanos employs a health nurse, and Marta González will soon retire.

This change in needs among the people does not end the interest in providing health related service. However, the focus has changed to programs such as that of HEPAC (Nogales) which now provides healthy meals to children, a program that once was provided through Compañeros en Misión. HEPAC also provides healthy meals for migrants, especially those being repatriated to México by the U.S.

Likewise, the Migrant Resource Center (MRC) and its partners in Agua Prieta provide healthy meals to migrant families, first aid, rehydration, and, if necessary, more extensive remedial care in various programs around the town. Several of MRC's partners provide cool or warm places for migrants to stay once they return, a service that assures a stabilization of people who had spent days in the dessert and in detention centers.

Since many resources were spent for about twenty-five years on developing a network of health promoters, that work continues at all sites. The promoters continue to teach classes to young mothers about pre-natal care of themselves, care of infants and of young children. For those of us in the U.S., such matters seem of no concern, but we must remember that communication with family is still difficult and young women often have no family close by for mentoring.

4. Drug and alcohol addiction

This issue of alcohol and drug addiction continues to be of considerable importance. Many of the young men and women of the Presbyterian Church, entered the church because their first experience with the church is with others who ministered to them when they were addicts and alcoholics. Rev. Roberto Mendoza, now serving Prince of Peace Church in Ciudad Juárez, testifies, "Before becoming a Christian, I was addicted, chained to alcohol and drugs, but, thanks be to God, Jesus rescued me from those chains. I'll never go back." He is one of the Mexican leaders who understands not all those who drink alcohol become alcoholics, but as for him that is past.

One hears these stories often in México as we do in the U.S.—pastors and church leaders who have been rescued or "saved" from the bonds of addiction who now minister to others. At one time these ministries were all there were. Today, that is changing and there are special centers like CRREDA in Agua Prieta that run a detox program, an Alcoholics and Narcotics Anonymous, and counseling service. Frontera de Cristo has partnered with them for this service which can more effectively minister to this ever present need. There is an atmosphere of joy at CRREDA among those who have overcome their addiction and who work with the program today. While the facility is far below the standards demanded of detox programs, the care is evidently generous and effective and the participants thankful.

While the focus of CRREDA is on addiction, a high priority is providing places to become engaged in service to others who have or may be going through much the same trials the patients have endured. So the CRREDA folks go to the desert to deliver water to water stations on migrant routes so persons preparing to cross the border can fill their bottles with safe water. The hope is that the migrants will have enough water to arrive at similar water stations established by Humane Borders on the U.S. side. As one participant said, "I'm learning not to make my life all about me. If I do that, I get depressed and drink and take drugs. I have something else to think about now—others."

5. *Sustainable Life Practices*

Subsistence life is common to the poor of México and even for many who have jobs, have settled and begun developing their own homes. A lost job can send the family into a tail spin of uncertainty and abject poverty because the family lacks a foundation of wealth.

In addition life in the desert regions, which is characteristic of the border lands in general, is difficult. As Rosario Viesca, wife of Pastor Jésus Gallegos, said, "Having come from Ciudad Chihuahua, we thought Tijuana was bad. When we went to Agua Prieta, my first thought was, 'How do people live? Nothing grows here.'"

Indeed! The desert is an unforgiving place and only the most adaptable survive, and the people who come to the border are usually from places with much more lush ecologies. Growing food back home was fairly easy and they had many people to teach them how. Growing food on the border looks nearly impossible and takes special skills.

Dougla Prieta Trabajan (DPT) is a center for educating people on building a Permaculture that combines agriculture and community. They provide skills training, family gardening education, and community building skills. Permaculture seeks to plant gardens in a manner suitable to the environment to take advantage of the ecological realities of one's neighborhood. In conjunction with building stronger communities, community gardening is encouraged to take as much advantage of common spaces (parks, donated property, church yards, and the like) as possible. DPT teaches people how to do all of this and encourages everyone to have a home garden and to participate in community gardens.

Miriam Maldonado, wife of the U.S. co-coordinator of Frontera de Cristo, has turned their front yard into a veritable jungle of vegetables and chicken yard taking advantage of the synergy between the chickens and the vegetables. The vegetables draw insects to the patch which the chickens eat. The chicken manure is high in nitrogen which enriches the ground. As the cycle continues, the ground will become richer. Mrs. Adams also puts the household garbage out to compost. Her project is a way of drawing attention to the possibilities, even in the desert, of growing one's own food.

Sometimes a sustainable system stretches from border to border as is the case with Just Coffee, a dream of Daniel Cifuentes and others of those who came from Chiapas. Having worked as a coffee farmer before coming to the border, Cifuentes wondered what could

Just Coffee Processing Facility, Agua Prieta

be done with coffee on the border. After some time of discussion, thinking and praying, the idea was hatched to create a coffee cooperative. Plans were developed and representatives from Agua Prieta went to Chiapas to recruit growers to the project. Having achieved success on that front, the agreement was to buy all a farmer's product at a price determined by the members. Some of the processing of the coffee harvest is done in Chiapas and when the beans are ready they are shipped to Agua Prieta where they are roasted, packaged and sent, for the most part, to churches in the U.S. for sale. The coffee is organically grown and processed and exceeds the requirements for Fair Trade status because not only do the farmers get a fair price for their beans, they also have their social security (pension and health insurance) paid for by the coop.

Most fair trade coffee brings the beans to the U.S. to be roasted, but Just Coffee is also roasted, packaged and shipped from México so more jobs are created. The roasting plant employees are paid double the Mexican minimum wage by decision of the coop members who do not want to create jealousy by earning much more than their brothers and sisters in the church or their neighbors.

The effect has been astounding. Growing sales from 10,000 pounds to nearly 60,000 pounds per year in ten years was remarkable given the marketing plan that connects the farmers and roasters with church members in the U.S. While most of the coffee is sold in Presbyterian churches, it is also sold in churches of other denominations. The coop has received grants from the PCUSA Women's Birthday Offering and from organizations of other denominations.

Just Coffee has benefited the communities where the farmers live by providing a steady income, new businesses, stronger cooperative spirit across denominational lines, and a more sustainable community. Tommy Bassett, who works with Just Coffee and directs Just Trade Centers, reported that over one-hundred persons have returned from the U.S. to their farms because of Just Coffee. The jobs created by the roasting plant in Agua Prieta have helped to bring stability to the Lily of the Valleys Presbyterian Church which now is seeking to start new churches and participating in mission trips to other regions in México.[48]

At Pasos de Fe a new ministry we would call an anti-recidivism program has begun at the community center, partnering with a man whose heart is committed to helping those who have been released from prison to escape the cycle of crime and hope to insulate them from returning to or being recruited by cartels. He does so by teaching them a trade and proclaiming the gospel thus linking a social need with one's need for spiritual salvation.

---

[48] For more about Just Coffee see the website http://www.justcoffee.org. Tommy Basset and Mark Adams have also written *Just Coffee: Caffeine with a Conscience*, which is available on the website. Also, see my article "More than Fair" (http://www.pcusa.org/news/2010/12/15/more-fair/) in Presbyterian News Service, December 2010, and "New Life at the Border" (http://presbyteriansonthefrontier.net/presby-today-article.pdf) in Presbyterians Today, January/February, 2011.

Policy Engagement

The U.S. government and the various states have had laws on the books regarding immigration for many years. The present federal law is little changed since the 1980s as discussed above. The main differences in terms of federal law have to do with enforcement. As already discussed, enforcement efforts have skyrocketed over the last sixteen plus years so that today, the U.S. border with México is one of the most militarized places on earth.

Despite federal efforts, the border states have had persons who have built a cottage industry of promoting the idea that the federal government is not doing anything to stop the flow of immigrants across the border. Texas, Arizona, New México and California all have passed laws that dealt with migrations into their states. Those laws have been understood by many as discriminatory not only towards undocumented Mexican migrants but also most persons of Latin American heritage.

However, the concern of border ministry is the human cost of the federal policy and the increased law enforcement by states. Most of the ministries do not do any overt lobbying of congress, but they do speak out on the issues of concern. Some find ways to draw attention of the tragedy of deaths in the desert that also draws attention to those who suffer health crises while crossing but are strong enough to survive.

In Douglas, AZ Frontera de Cristo cooperates with a vigil started by Roman Catholic nuns. Volunteers have made simple white wooden crosses each of which bears the name of someone who has died while crossing the border. One wonders about each of the names of the several hundred who have died in Arizona deserts alone. Where is the person from? Whose parents are his or hers? Did s/he have children or even grandchildren? Does the family know about them? But one certainly asks those questions and more for persons who lacked a name and the cross bears the words "No Identificado/a".

Empathy requires one to respond with more than prayers as at the vigil that takes place on the U.S. side along the road for persons going into México. So most of the ministries seek to have delegations from the U.S. learn about the border, why people migrate, what is happening in U.S. policy that were it changed, life for the migrant would not be so dangerous.

Beyond border education, some who serve in border ministry positions and many who volunteer, become engaged in the attempt to change border policy and immigration law. While the uninitiated may not see a difference, border policy and immigration law are two different things. Immigration law is written to deal with all migration into the U.S. from all over the world and deals with many arcane subjects like types of visas, requirements for immigration, whether or not to tether visas to employers, quotas for various countries, and so on. Border policy deals almost totally with securing the borders and dealing with undocumented persons who have crossed the borders. It includes how and where to build border fences, necessary clothing, boots, surveillance equipment, detention facilities, and so on. All that Border Patrol and immigration officials who work along the border do has to do with the flow of immigrants across the border, detecting and apprehending them, and processing them.

Seeing the policies as unjust and dangerous, some chose to advocate for changes to the law so that they will be more humane. Especially in Arizona, certain PBM personnel and many volunteers work for changes in the law in the state houses and in the U.S. congress and White House. They participate in everything from marches to visiting legislators. Most important is the sharing of information and experiences at home in their churches.

Violence

Bridging the work of Frerichs and McReynolds, the board of Proyecto Amistad pursued a clearer vision for the ministry eventually identifying an evangelistic response to the violence. Believing that providing a ministry to children was the best means of reducing violence in the future, the ministry searched out materials to use in teaching the children about Christ and provide them a foundation to resist violence and practice peace.

The choice does not receive universal support because the AMO curriculum is quite chauvinistic and fundamentalist, however, the INPM is both of those as well. Because McReynold and his wife, Francelia, and Medina are each immersed in the concerns of women, the training of teachers has focused on the goals of Amistad not on the materials, and that training colors how the teachers are trained and the material interpreted. As Medina said,

We focus that God created all children whole and God wants them to overcome their difficulties and prepare for their futures. Children experience a lot of abuse by various persons in the family. Children cry about the abuse and they share with the pastors and teachers because they can't do so with their mothers or fathers. We provide a sanctuary for the children. We tell them that if God loves them and created them whole, then God wants them to have a good life and gives them the ability to be what God desires for them. It is a simple message. Then we teach them the Bible and how Jesus wants them to practice peace not kill each other.

I was privileged to attend two Children's Day (a national holiday in many countries) celebrations at two of the churches for the Club Amistad. The children played games, ate, and worshipped. They know their Bibles, exude confidence, and respond readily to questions about the Bible and theology. The parents also come. The teachers and parents are taught that God does not want them to use violence with children and that the only way to become a peaceful society is to find peaceful ways to discipline and, no matter what, to show love.

The teachers all have to be trained both in the vision of Club Amistad and in the Bible and materials. "Nobody assumes that because a person is an adult that she or he is automatically a teacher. The training is arduous and required," said Medina, "but the impact on the children and their families is obvious. We hope that impact will be felt in the future." Today, there are more than 500 children across México engaged in Club Amistad.

Chapter 4: Challenges to Maintaining the Binational Relationship and Mission

Paternalism still lives

While much has been learned about overcoming paternalism, the challenge is still a constant in the work. Every new person, whether Mexican or U.S., has to be taught the binational mutual ministry model and then how to listen perhaps more carefully than in most other contexts. As David Thomas, and his wife, Susan, formerly co-coordinators of Compañeros en Misión and then liaisons to México, said, "While the border personnel and church members came to understand what we were trying to do, I really never felt like the leadership of the INPM did. Then we had the problem fairly regularly of some Mexican pastors, who were under constant economic stress like the rest of the

Mexicans, taking opportunity to garner favors from U.S. delegation members. One can understand why this happened, but it was our job to try to overcome it."

The Thomases report the good news that despite that Mexican churches were not mission oriented and seldom sent mission delegations elsewhere, some progress had been made. For example, the Presbytery of Southern Kansas made annual trips to Agua Prieta where they were joined by persons from the Lily of the Valleys Church and they then went on to Caborca (about four hours to the west) where together with the people in Caborca, they did building projects, Bible Schools and spent time with each other. Today, the church of Agua Prieta partially supports the pastor of the church in Caborca.

Amistad in Nuevo Laredo today continues to support church development at times far from home, such as Puerto Vallarta nearly 1300 miles southwest and Acuña about 300 miles west. While this work began primarily as the work of Amistad, today the people of México are more fully engaged with little work from the former U.S partners who are afraid to go.

One can hear stories about the Mexicans coming to U.S. churches to do mission work, help with evangelism, or with Vacation Bible Schools in Spanish language neighborhoods. Bill Soldwisch tells the story of a California church that came to paint a church in México. While painting the ceiling, one of the U.S. young people said, "Our church ceiling needs painting but we'd never paint it." One of the Mexicans heard and understood the comment and volunteered that his church would go paint it. Not long after the California church had a painted ceiling. Sometimes the mutuality just happens.

Nearly everyone I spoke with reported that the boards function much better today with a better understanding of what must be done to assure good communication and to avoid the habits of paternalism. Thus everyone is still learning to live in the model. Other examples of this sort of new mission ventures can be found in the previous chapters.

Learning to live in the model of mutuality

1. The rich and thus more powerful

Our world is impacted by money in every avenue of life. Even in the U.S where most are well off in comparison to the majority of the world, we recognize that money creates power. As income inequality becomes a larger issue in our nation, that fact is felt even more strongly. When we have two nations with an extensive border with one side in poverty and the other wealthy, the power of wealth looms over everything. Looking across the border from a mountain top in El Paso, the line between wealth and poverty is clear as is the line between the powerful and the not so powerful as that between the U.S. and México. In public affairs and international relations, what the U.S. wants, México nearly always agrees to.

The two churches we have been looking at experience the same thing. The Mexican church knows we have money and they know most of the work that has been done in the border regions could never have been done without the aid of U.S Presbyterians. They constantly thank God for our generosity with our time and our resources. That dynamic is problematic. Their thankfulness often surrenders to an attitude of deference. If the Mexican church gets the sense that the U.S. church wants something, it will often defer without expressing their misgivings—a perpetuation of paternalism.

Likewise, their sense of gratitude leads the Mexican church to feelings of inferiority, something most in the U.S. do not wish. However, this is a human condition that we even talk about in our political discourse —"Welfare", we say "creates dependence." Whether welfare actually does create dependence is arguable, but those who contribute their wealth have to be careful and clear that their wealth is a gift from God that they willing share without strings. Even so, we live in the real world, not an ideal one and the reality is that those who receive gifts seldom think the gifts can be without strings.

The challenge is on both sides to learn how to recognize the considerable gifts of both churches. The INPM, as David Thomas pointed out, has considerable gifts in evangelism and knows how to do it well. The U.S. church has never asked for their assistance in teaching us how to do it. "No matter what area of church life, (those in the U.S.) think we know how to do it best. We have a sort of arrogance," says Thomas.

2. The poorer church and its struggle for dignity

Poverty has its own psychology. When one is poor, one feels deeply inadequate and powerless. When one interviews those who live in abject poverty, as I have in México and Colombia, one senses the incredible dignity of the people that lies beneath the surface and the struggle they are undergoing to be able to hold their head high despite their poverty. An important element in that struggle is the sense, "If I just had money, I'd be able to solve my problem." Those of us who have always had adequate resources have difficulty empathizing with this attitude.

The INPM is conscious of that concept. The work that Saúl Tijerina did to lead the INPM to the table in PBM was a phenomenal exertion for this very reason— the Mexican leadership was not sure that a truly binational mutual mission was possible given the history of missions. One of the challenges reported by his colleague Jerry Stacy was that Dr. Tijerina had to help the INPM overcome the reticence of being seen as the weaker partner. After all, the whole point of the missionary moratorium was for the INPM to mature and become independent. The last thing it wanted to do was to appear as if it were going begging once more.

That explains the careful wording of the "A New Relation in Mission". It had to assure that the maturity and independence of the INPM was recognized and create an understanding of mutuality and interdependence not of dependence. Despite the structuring of PBM to assure mutuality and cooperation, it continues to be difficult for the Mexican board members to overcome their tendency to defer to the wishes of those with the financial resources. It is equally difficult for those with the resources to recognize when this is happening and to avoid appearing to force their ideas on the partners.

3. The Gifts That Cross the Borders

Everyone involved in border ministry, Mexican and U.S., recognize the incredible gifts that each church has. We clearly share three gifts: faith and love for the good news of God, hospitality and generosity.

The Mexican people are very aware that those from the U.S. who come to visit them, work with them, and serve among them could be doing something else like going to Puerto Vallarta or Cancún on vacation. They recognize the cost of mission trips and the sacrifice of time and energy, emotional and physical. They reciprocate generously welcoming U.S. delegations into their churches and their homes.

Church services often are altered to provide for translation making them longer, a necessity whenever there is neither equipment nor a talented person to provide simultaneous translation. The Mexicans enjoy singing hymns familiar in both cultures in Spanish and English. U.S. delegation members enjoy the cultural experience of usually vibrant and energetic worship, amazed that in the Presbyterian Church in México, few men stand silent during the singing of hymns as many men in the U.S. do. One delegation member told me, "They almost make me want to sing." He didn't think he could sing so he did not. In México, the people sing joyfully even when they sing off key. "The Bible", one music leader told me, "says make a joyful noise, not sing on key."

Most mission delegations are welcomed into the community and often into the homes of Mexicans. When meals are served to delegations, an arrangement is made for financing the meals that is mostly behind the scenes through the coordinators. I discovered early on that offering to pay for the hospitality of our hosts was insulting to them. Despite their meager resources, hospitality is a mark of dignity and a matter of culture that is uncompromising. Reciprocation can only come with in-kind experiences like providing the host with similar hospitality in our homes or a gift that is not monetary— a photo of one's family, a gift for the home, an album of one's church or family, but not money.

It is hard to distinguish generosity and hospitality. Only a truly generous spirit can be genuinely hospitable, otherwise the hospitality seems inauthentic. Randy Campbell tells of the wonderful experiences of the Mexican Presbyterians in the homes of Presbyterians in Phoenix and their testimony of feeling truly welcomed. By sharing in such experiences we come to recognize the profound faith of our brothers and sisters across the border.

We also learn about our faith and love for the good news of God. The INPM is notably more conservative than the PCUSA in issues of doctrine and social values. Mexican Presbyterians do not believe in drinking alcohol or smoking. Those from the southern regions of México are far more conservative in dress than those along the border. As Rosario Viesca told me,

> The people from the south come here and wonder why we do not wear dresses and think at first we are immodest, but it is not long until they understand that dresses can be far more immodest here than pants. We came to learn that the biblical injunction against women wearing men's clothing is that I cannot wear clothes made for men, but I can wear slacks and

jeans made for women. We do teach modesty but modesty has to be practical. Wearing dresses where the wind blows like crazy makes no sense.

Their own experiences have taught the Mexican Presbyterians something about how culture affects one's view of certain principles. One way we share is understanding that loving God and having faith is not locked into our cultural understandings. At least for those along the border, Mexican Presbyterians have come to accept what they consider to be inappropriate dress among U.S. girls and women. When PBM began, female mission delegations members were almost commanded not to wear sleeveless blouses, shorts or pants. Today, even the women in the churches in México wear such clothing having learned even people of faith can act modestly, even if their clothing is not according to the old standards.

The use of alcohol and smoking was also an issue, and while in some cases still is, Mexican Presbyterians for the most part have experienced the deep faith of the U.S. Presbyterians who smoke and drink alcohol. Of course, we honor their prohibition by not doing so while among them, in their homes, their churches and their communities.

4. The Affirmation of Diversity

Depending on where one is in México, the congregations are made up of a distinctly diverse range of genetics. Intermarriage of the races has been common among Mexicans from its colonial days. While there is still a prejudice in favor of lighter skin color, the churches are filled with people bearing the genetic characteristics of the native peoples, Africans, Europeans, and to the astonishment of many, Asians. In the church they are all welcomed with equanimity.

Most U.S. Presbyterians who go to border ministry sites are probably comfortable with such an inclusion of various ethnic and racial backgrounds, yet U.S. churches continue to be segregated. In the U.S. we have ethnic, national and racially segregated congregations. The PCUSA even has an emphasis to start and develop such churches: Korean, Congolese, Cambodian, Spanish Language, Chinese, and so on. In the U.S. we even segregate further by refusing to have worship that honors all generational preferences and transform our worship into a genuinely international, cross cultural, and intergenerational experience. Instead U.S. Anglo congregations stick doggedly to Eurocentric hymnody and liturgy.

The INPM had its roots in the Eurocentric model but have given witness to becoming indigenous, as have many of our sister denominations in other nations. Their services continue to include hymns of mission origins like "Amazing Grace", "God of Grace and God of Glory", "The Church's One Foundation" and the like, but the services also include songs sung to traditional Mexican music and to contemporary music. Perhaps, we can learn from our sisters and brothers around the world how to sacrifice our preference for the preferences of others to create a worship experience hospitable to all as a way of affirming our diversity.

The challenge is not one sided. There is a sticking point or two in this soup between the INPM and the

PCUSA. The PCUSA ordains women to be pastors, elders and deacons. The INPM does not. The PCUSA has now voted to permit the ordination of sexually active gay and lesbian persons to those positions. The INPM adamantly opposes that decision which has led to a grievous cancellation by the INPM of our thirty year old denominational partnership and over one-hundred years of informal relationship. Few have any hope that a formal relationship will ever happen again.

Chapter 5: What Prospects and Challenges Lie Ahead for PBM?

As reported above in Chapter 3, the INPM voted August 19, 2011 to severe relationships with the PCUSA over the issue of ordination of gay and lesbian persons.[49] On August 16 four members of the PCUSA GA and Mission staffs—Rev. Gradye Parsons, Stated Clerk; Rev. Dr. Hunter Farrell, Director of PC(USA) World Mission; María Arroyo, Area Coordinator for Latin America and the Caribbean, PC(USA) World Mission and David Thomas, Regional Liaison for México, PC(USA) World Mission— met with the executive committee of the INPM to discuss the reaction of the INPM to the decision of the PCUSA.

---

[49] Much of the following is based on a report written by former PCUSA Liaison to México, Dave Thomas, to the México Mission Network of the PCUSA and an extensive interview with him.

The result was a recommendation to the legislative session of the General Assembly of the INPM, as David Thomas reported,

> The executive committee's declaration at the special G.A. legislative session included a proposal that the partnership with PC(USA) be temporarily suspended until the next regular meeting of the INPM's G.A., which is scheduled in July, 2012, in Monterrey, Nuevo León (northern México). It also recommended that a sentence in the church's *Book of Order* referring to the INPM-PC(USA) partnership be removed, and that between now and next July, the matter of Amendment 10-A be analyzed and studied, with results and a recommendation to be presented at the meeting in Monterrey. (See footnote 49)

Several motions were made but not adopted, however, a motion was made and overwhelmingly passed to immediately break relations with a provision to reconsider the decision should Amendment 10-A be rescinded by the PCUSA. The decision threw the future of PBM in doubt by severing the binational relationship on which PBM was founded.

Sadly, most of the GA meetings of the INPM take place in southern and central México creating two problems for the pastors and elders along the U.S. and México border. First, the trip to GA is long and tiring requiring days away from one's ministry. Second, responsibility for the expenses of the trip are that of the persons going and include auto expenses, meals and lodging. Few of the northern pastors or elders attended this significant meeting so the views of the border presbyteries were not well represented.

Adding to the other hardships, was that this meeting was supposed to be a consultation of the role of women in the church and the possibility of ordination for women. That issue was dealt with and a motion prohibiting the ordination of women passed. The issue regarding the relationship with the PCUSA was not on the original agenda and thus an unannounced business item. When the item came up for consideration, it was clear to observers that few commissioners read the amendment and thus voted on hearsay that claimed it approved the ordination of gay and lesbian persons. The way the amendment reads no mention is made of gay and lesbian persons. Instead, it returns the authority for determining the worthiness of a candidate for ministry to the presbyteries and church sessions.

The boards of the PBM ministry immediately asked the Executive Committee of INPM for some explanation for what they could do in their relationships with their boards and PCUSA presbyteries, synods and congregations. The answer was that as long as the U.S. congregation, presbytery, or synod rejected 10-A, the relationships could be maintained, however, they must cease immediately relationships with congregations, presbyteries and synods, or ministers who refused to reject 10-A.

The INPM churches and ministers along the border did not automatically agree with the INPM decision despite how they felt about 10-A. As Chris McReynolds pointed out, the church of México has two distinct cultures. One is the one in the north that has experienced considerable interaction with U.S. presbyterians and the one in the central and southern parts of México where the churches have little experience of the U.S. presbyterians. he stated, "While the engagement along the border has been a good and deepening experience for the northern presbyterians, there has been almost no filtering of that experience to the south."

Mexican leaders along the border have differing perspectives on this question although few openly state support for the ordination of gay and lesbian persons. However, when asked about the severance of the partnership, they nearly all expressed dismay and worry about the future of PBM and most have expressed concerns to the executive committee of the INPM over the decisions and asked for a way to continue the ministry.

Of course, PCUSA ministers, congregations, presbyteries and synods are also not of one mind, as represented by Presbytery of San Diego which almost immediately voted to reject 10-A. This opened the door for both Presbytery of San Diego and Presbytery of Northwest México to establish a relationship with Pueblos Hermanos and keep the ministry alive with the cooperation of Baja Presbyterian Missions. As Mexican Co-coordinator Rev. Enrique Romero of Pueblos Hermanos stated,

> We recently began to have a new relationship with San Diego presbytery occurring after the breaking of national relations. The national decision brought new opportunities for dialogue

with the Presbytery of San Diego. We have had a series of discussions for uniting our forces in the evangelistic work. The local church has told us that it does not want to close the doors locally speaking as border churches. We tell it that if it agrees with the INPM then we are able to have a relation. Without the support of the Presbytery, the resources of Pueblos Hermanos will be very low. So in July we made an agreement between the Presbyteries of San Diego and the Presbytery of the Northwest (México).

While things moved smoothly for Pueblos Hermanos and the opening for continued relations clear, other ministries did not have it so easy. Other border presbyteries and synods and many congregations and pastors that had been in relationships with the ministries were not willing to revoke their own vote on 10-A (a matter of record for the presbyteries) raising the question, "Is there another way?"

The Executive Committee came back with a way to work around the problem. If the ministries formed themselves as non-profit agencies independent of the INPM and the PCUSA, then the INPM ministers, congregations and presbyteries could relate to the non-profit but not directly to the PCUSA. Thus the ministries followed this path. The question was still in play regarding what had been the oversight committee and board that worked with all six ministries.

The directive of the INPM left little room for a binational committee similar to that of PBM over the last twenty-nine years because the INPM was an important player in that work. The question was whether or not each ministry would be independent with no functioning committee overseeing and facilitating the work of the six ministries, and how might such a committee function?

On March 1, 2013, the U.S. representatives met and approved a plan for moving forward. No longer able to be binational, the decision was made following a year of consultation between representatives of the six ministries and PC(USA) World Mission to form a new organizing board and ministry to be named Presbyterian Border Region Outreach (PBRO). The Mission statement of the new entity is:

> Living out the Gospel of Jesus Christ holistically on both sides of the U.S.- México Border, in partnership with other faith organizations and non-profits to reduce poverty and violence in the Border Region.[50]

The document adopted by the board goes on to say:

> PBRO will be an umbrella for ministry sites to help facilitate our holistic approach in addressing root causes of poverty and promoting reconciliation in cultures of violence. In all of our work we are accountable first to our Lord Jesus Christ, and through the Holy Spirit to one another, always responding to God's image in our neighbor.

---

[50] See appendix C.

One can readily see that the mission statement and the purpose statement focus attention on historic concerns of U.S. Presbyterians concerns. Poverty has always been a primary reason that U.S. Presbyterians were drawn to work on the border which led to the creation of community centers, health ministries, educational programs, drug and alcohol addiction programs, and many of the numerous other ministries. The new piece is the focus is on "promoting reconciliation in cultures of violence".[51]

Clearly, this is a binational concern with which Mexican Presbyterians are engaged.[52] But what about the INPM's most ardent concern for evangelism and church development? The plan is to encourage each border ministry to decide on its goals and to focus where it sees its ministry has the greatest needs. As Rev. Nelsen of University Presbyterian Church, El Paso, and president of PBRO said, "Evangelism had to be an area we could not directly address any longer. That had to be left to the Mexican Presbyteries and the ministry boards to decide how to do church development." Clearly, several sites have a strong emphasis in evangelism and church development, and as far as the U.S. and Mexican board members decide to place emphasis there, the resources will also flow in that direction. Pueblos Hermanos, Compañeros en Misión, and Proyecto Amistad already

---

[51] PCUSA World Mission established three goals for its work around the world. The first was to seek ways to reduce poverty and the second to promote reconciliation in cultures of violence and the third was proclamation of the gospel (evangelism).

[52] Most of what follows comes from conversations with Rev. John Nelsen and Rev. Mark Adams regarding the work of PBRO.

have a very strong emphasis on evangelism and church development.

As of this writing the new facilitator for PBRO, Omar Chan, has been assigned and will be in place by June, 2014. He has experience as a mission co-worker in Guatemala where he is finishing his work in preparation to moving to El Paso where the new office will be located. He is also married to Amanda Craft, a mission worker whose responsibility is the Regional Representative for México and Guatemala. Along with the PBRO board, the facilitator will:

- Enlist existing ministry site boards to join in implementing the new mission
- Enlist existing PCUSA Mission co-workers
- "Re-Introduce" PBM as PBRO within the PCUSA, Synods, Presbyteries and churches.
- Submit Articles about PBRO to Presbyterian Missions publications, others
- Appeal to Current Donor Base for Funds; Expand to Potential Donors
- Research, Identify, Develop Relationships and Come Alongside Existing Social Service Agencies in the Border Region who Share our Mission
- Encourage/Recruit US Churches to Donate, to Visit, to Work with these Agencies
- Prepare information packets for visiting groups and partners
- Facilitator will ensure Line 202 must have $20,000 in it (funding to ministry sites)[53]

---

[53] I followed the capitalization in the board document and made no other corrections.

Needless to say, the ministry sites will continue to encourage the INPM partners in their efforts at church development and design their own plans for alleviating poverty and violence. Proyecto Amistad has provided one model for addressing violence through Christian education and is offering training and resourcing for other ministries and regions of México to engage. Chris McReynolds has recently resigned his position as co-coordinator of Amistad to commit full time to development of Club Amistad for the INPM in all of México. While broadening his work, he does not see himself as abandoning work with Amistad but increasing that work.

As PBRO gears up Mr. Chan will be responsible for working with the various ministries to identify ways, means, and partners to address the culture of violence in their region of México and the U.S., although violence in U.S. border towns is incredibly low. It is possible that the ministries will incorporate Club Amistad approaches to violence, but also likely each will find a unique way to address the problem.

Conclusion

When I began working on this project nobody was predicting that the PCUSA would decide to permit the ordination of sexually active homosexual persons to office in the church. Nor could anyone predict for sure how our mission partners around the globe would react. There were some good guesses but each national church reacted in their own interests and out of their own theologies which, like that of the PCUSA, are evolving.

The INPM still does not ordain women nor does it permit churches to ordain women as deacons or elders, a point of disagreement between the INPM and the PCUSA since the 1950s. Yet, a strong movement within the INPM is afoot to change that but will probably not come until a leadership change at the executive level. As Dr. Pazos explained, "The INPM is more Episcopal than the PCUSA, more centralized. So everything begins in México City and ultimately ends there. Presbytery committees decide where ministers will go with only some input from the churches. Presbytery committees decide where new churches will be started." To be fair the presbytery committees are made up of ministers and elders, but the input that we are accustomed to in the U.S. is not as common in the INPM. Control at the national level is much stronger and those who implement the policies of the General Assembly are far fewer than in PCUSA. Women are virtually voiceless.

It appears that one of the basic principles of the "A New Relation in Mission" adopted by the INPM and then included as part of the joint understanding was violated in the decision of the INPM to severe relationships. That principle was:

> Therefore, we respect other churches and missionary entities and, by the same token, we ask for respect of the particular expression of our understanding of Biblical doctrine and the execution of our task as well as the culture and idiosyncrasy of our Country.

The movement towards more openness is slow and plodding wherever one is but the INPM is far more conservative than the PCUSA has been in most of the last century on issues regarding women and certainly on most social issues. One reason pointed out by Rick Lane, member of board of Proyecto Amistad, may be that the INPM has been for most of its history a persecuted church.[54] For most of México's history a Protestant was passed over for employment, promotion or laid off in preference for a Roman Catholic, a practice becoming

---

[54] Interview in SanAntonio May, 2012.

less common with the globalizing of the economy. Most U.S., Asian, and European businesses are only interested in work habits and qualifications.

During my first summer at FdC, there were reports of Protestant Christians being beaten for being Protestant. In no way does that mean the Roman Catholic authorities condone such violence. However, as Roberto Medina reported, "Recently, the youth gangs have targeted Protestant churches, robbing them during worship." Indeed, while I was visiting Nuevo Laredo and Puerta del Cielo Church, the people were asked to stay and fill out a survey to see if they were able and willing to have their contributions electronically transferred because of recent robberies at worship services. Mr. Medina does not believe such behavior is in any way condoned by the authorities but it shows the religious divide in the nation as none of the churches that had been robbed were Roman Catholic, many of which would have had far more money and even higher priced cars to take.

A common approach to threat is to become protective and to behave more conservatively. Even the PC(USA) feels that pressure. Loss of membership is blamed on liberalism although surveys do not bear out that claim. Congregations that are declining become more entrenched and less courageous, and neither the PC(USA) nor our congregations have suffered persecution. Lane suggested that the persecution of the INPM has created a context for being more conservative and protectionist. One cannot easily draw any conclusions from such an observation except to say, he may have a good point to be considered. Only the Mexicans can verify his hypothesis.

Another issue that Chris McReynolds pointed out and is confirmed by nearly everyone I spoke with is that the people on the border and those from the U.S. who have participated in PBM work are committed to the work, have grown to know, respect and trust one another. However, that same level of engagement has not reached into the whole of the INPM or the PC(USA). The sad truth is that despite PC(USA) World Mission's spending large sums of money to tell its story to the churches, only a small percentage of Presbyterians can talk intelligently about a single mission partnership of the PC(USA). Whether I speak about our work in Colombia or México, the resounding response is, "I didn't know we were doing that sort of thing." I once heard a disgruntled pastor report on the GA he had attended as a commissioner. He had nothing to say about anything except the legislative agenda mostly focusing on the decision to send a *Book of Order* amendment to change ordination standards, a decision he opposed. When I asked him about the number of new missionaries commissioned and other celebrations of mission, he could not respond. Was he out of the room? Did he just shut out all the good news? Apparently so, because the GA always includes incredible stories about our mission work, churches with unique ministries and successes of ministries across the nation and around the world.

Perhaps the biggest challenge to the church universal is how little we know about one another which leads to the perpetuation of prejudices and ambivalence. It is clear that despite the formal break between the PC(USA) and the INPM, the pastors and people along the border have a sincere desire to maintain relations with one another and continue the work. Therefore, they have energetically sought ways to do so, a result of which is that each board has joined the PBRO as an organization and has representatives to attend its meetings. Each ministry board has thought through its work and moved ahead with renewed vision and plans.

The good news from the border is that Presbyterians are still working across the border to tell the good news of Jesus Christ and to demonstrate the love of God in amazing ways. Through that work the love of God's people flourishes with its sometimes strident differences forcing us to reflect on our own lapses of faithfulness and love for sister and brother.

That work is helped in El Paso by the board of Pasos de Fe having the support of the Presbytery of Chihuahua whose moderator, Rev. Filipe Barandiarán, is also a pastor in Ciudad Juárez and now pastoring the Spanish language service at University PC in El Paso. Similar close relationships between the pastors on both sides developed over many years of service together, which leads them to continue working together despite the national church decisions. While the PCUSA and the INPM will no longer have a binational partnership, the border ministries are now reorganized as non-profits and continue to have boards representing the churches on both sides of the border. The commitments to continuing the work are high and new ministries as narrated above are continuing.

Rev. Nelsen says, "The energy of the PBRO board is on a scale of one-ten about a four, but that is much better than last year. Once Mr. Chan arrives, we expect the energy to increase considerably, but the future looks quite bright today."

Mrs. Maria Arroyo, Area Coordinator for Latin America and the Caribbean, seconds the optimism, saying that there are "many positive signs for the future of the bi-national work, perhaps, most important is the number of Mexican Presbyterians interested in continuing their work with U.S. Presbyterians." She believes that the reorganization of PBRO and of each of the Border Ministry sites bodes well for the overall vision. The challenges lie mostly in the viability of a few of the sites that have struggles and will continue to struggle with financial viability. Another important positive is that there is enthusiasm among both Mexican and U.S. Presbyterians for the work to be done and each site seems to be making renewed efforts.

Needless to say a major concern is raising the funds to continue the ministries and provide adequate staff. Frontera de Cristo and Pueblos Hermanos have prospered because both have had consistent staffing for many years and a well developed constituency capable of building and maintaining financial and physical presence on the border. Sadly, the physical presence in the form of mission delegations from U.S. churches has dwindled because of fears raised by the terrorist attacks of 9/11, the news reports of the murders, and cartel and gang violence in Mexico. Several of the ministries had depended on that aspect of their ministry which was addressed above.

"With the Facilitator for PBRO we have opportunity to do evaluative conversations at each site to determine the resources available and the vision of each site for the future. As for PBRO, we want to focus its work on poverty among women and children and seeking resolution to violence. That will mean reaching out to other denominational ministries and para-ecclesial groups concerned with the same issues." In Mrs. Arroyo's opinion, each of the site boards will be finding differing ways to work with their constituencies to continue the work that allows for a range of options depending on the partnerships. The Mexicans have to find ways that avoid a conflict with the decisions of their denomination.

So what of the binational character of the ministry? Mrs. Arroyo replied, "We are presently working with other prospective partners in Mexico including the Communion of Presbyterians and Reformed Churches of Mexico and the Theological Community of Mexico City, D.F." The Communion is made up of some clergy and churches that have chosen to leave the INPM because of its stance against the ordination of women and other theological issues. Several of the clergy are women who received ordination before or in protest to the decision to prohibit the ordination of women.

With the new partners and the continuing commitment of the Presbyterians on both sides of the border, Mrs. Arroyo feels confident about the future despite not knowing what shape it will take. However, with nearly everyone I spoke there is certainty of the promise of Romans 6:28, "We know that in all things

God works for the good of those who love him, who have been called according to his purpose."

Looking ahead is possible because we feel suitably grounded, so I wish to conclude with a statement by Rev. Enrique Romero who has served nearly twenty-five years with Pueblos Hermanos. In the following words, I believe he pays homage to the mission work of U.S. Presbyterians and demonstrates the love and appreciation the people of the INPM have for the PCUSA. While Pastor Romero agrees with the decision of the INPM to break the binational relationship, he is joyful that an opening was left for continuing the work of Pueblos Hermanos. He also articulates how the work in México is connected to the work in the U.S and the work of the PC(USA) in Korea, indeed all that PC(USA) World Mission does in the world.

> I believe the meaning of bi-nationality is biblical. The Bible continues to be what is most important because it shows forth order and discipline for the church. I believe that we have a debt to the National Presbyterian Church of the U.S. because it taught us a beautiful doctrine— the Westminster Catechism. When I think of the Korean Church, which also provides us a lot of help, and was also developed by missionaries from the U.S.and has shown us the places where U.S. missionaries were buried and which they protect and revere. The cemetery is a place of honor and respect, a place of testimony and gratitude. It is so reverent because they were servant saints who went there to serve and die

but, here, because they were close to their native land, they returned and so México lacks these places of remembering the important events that have happened here. Many saints came forsaking their lives, their time, their money, their talents, to come to give all to the church of México. I believe that as Mexicans we do not forget, but we must make sure the church of North America knows we love it, that it is a church we remember fondly. México would not have known the Gospel if it were not for the testimony of the Presbyterian Church of the U.S. I know there are other denominations we love, but it has given us a beautiful doctrine and a marvelous Bible. We ought to be grateful for all that they did for México.

BIBLIOGRAPHY

Barrett, David; George Thomas Kurian, and Todd M. Johnson . <u>The World Christian Encyclopedia</u>. (Oxford University Press 1982, 2001)

Brackenridge, R. Douglas and Garcia-Treto, Francisco O. <u>Iglesia Presbiteriana: A History of Presbyterians and Mexican Americans in the Southwest.</u> Second Edition. (Trinity University Press, 1987)

Garcia-Treto, Francisco O. and Brackenridge, R. Douglas. "Hispanic Presbyterians: Life in Two Cultures", <u>The Diversity of Discipleship</u>, edited by Milton J. Coalter, et. al. (Westminster/John Knox Press, 1991), pp. 257-279.

Hegeman, Cornelius. <u>Mission to the People and Church Maintenance: The Origin and Development of Presbyterian and Reformed Churches and Missions in the Caribbean and Latin America (1528-1916)</u>. (American University of Biblical Studies, Atlanta, 2002)

Stacy, Jerry. <u>25 Years of Presbyterian Border Ministry</u>, (Self-Published)

Stacy, Gerald F. ed. "From Stranger to Neighbor", *Church and Society*. May/June 1982. PCUS and UPC, Washington, DC.

Numerous documents provided by PBM and the historical archives of PCUSA.

Appendices

Apendix A (See next page)

A NEW RELATION IN JOINT MISSION

INTRODUCTION

As the National Presbyterian Church of Mexico we confess our faith and hope
in God the Redeemer before the different churches and missionary entities
scattered throughout the world.

We believe that the Universal Church is made up of people of every tongue,
race and nation, to whom the message of reconciliation of God with the
sinner through Jesus Christ, as well as that of reconciliation of man with
his fellow man has been entrusted through the Gospel.

Therefore, those of us who make up the National Presbyterian Church of Mexico
rejoice in the fact that we belong to that great family of God, and thus we
declare that, based on the love of Christ, we join those who wish to make
Christ known to the world as the only Saviour of sinners.

God has ordained in His Church, as He has stated in His Word in Romans 12:6–8,
1 Corinthians 12:12 and 28, and Ephesians 4:11, 12, apostles, teachers,
preachers, evangelistics, etc. for the building up of the Body of Christ.

We believe the mission of the Church to be one of partnership and that,
therefore, as believers, we owe each one to the other, even if we live in
different parts of the world.

Therefore, in our fraternal relations with churches and missionary entities
from all the countries of earth, we join, joyfully and willingly, in a common
effort of aid and mutual cooperation to fulfil the mission of God in a world
which is shaken up and in need of the Gospel of Jesus Christ.

Because of this, and as a basis of those relations, we present the following:

DECLARATION OF THEOLOGICAL PRINCIPLES

1. WE BELIEVE in the sovereignty of God as Maker, Owner and Sustainer of
everything that exists and we acknowledge him as the only Lord of
conscience.

2. WE BELIEVE in the deity and humanity of Jesus Christ and we acknowledge
him as the Only Begotten Son of God and Redeemer of humankind.

3. WE BELIEVE in the Holy Spirit as Guide and Comforter of men and we
acknowledge his regenerating and purifying work in the life of human-
beings and His permanent presence in the life of the believers and of
the Church.

4. WE BELIEVE in the Holy Trinity: Father, Son and Holy Spirit and we
acknowledge the three persons as one God, equal in holiness, power
and glory.

5. WE BELIEVE in the Bible as written revelation and in its plenary inspiration by the power of the Holy Spirit and we acknowledge it as the only
rule of Christian faith and practice.

6. WE BELIEVE that man is a sinner by nature and unable to reach salvation
on his own merits and we acknowledge that he urgently needs Jesus Christ
as Saviour and Lord.

-2-

7. WE BELIEVE that the Universal Church is the Body of Christ, of whom He is the Head, and we acknowledge that the National Presbyterian Church of Mexico is part of that Body.

8. WE BELIEVE that the primary mission of the Church is to glorify God and that its task is the proclamation of the Gospel for the integral redemption of man and we acknowledge that there is only one Gospel, the Gospel of Jesus Christ.

9. WE BELIEVE that the Confession of Faith, the Westminster Catechisms and the Apostles' Creed are doctrinal symbols of the National Presbyterian Church of Mexico and we acknowledge that its doctrine is expressed satisfactorily based in the Holy Scriptures.

10. WE BELIEVE that the National Presbyterian Church of Mexico has reached her maturity and autonomy and we acknowledge its Constitution, Discipline, Liturgy and Order of Worship as the norms that govern its organization and life.

THEREFORE, we declare these THEOLOGICAL PRINCIPLES to be the determining basis of faith, of the work and of the relationships that the National Presbyterian Church of Mexico establishes with other ecclesiastical bodies and missionary entities.

ADMINISTRATIVE PRINCIPLES

WHEREAS we have been made partakers of the heavenly calling which bestows on us the privilege of enjoying the life of fullness of the Triune God through our Lord Jesus Christ, and which imposes on us the need to be his co-workers in the evangelistic task;

WHEREAS the Holy Spirit has distributed his gifts in the Church with the richness and diversity as well as with the consequent responsibility of each one in particular and all as a whole for the fulfillment of His will;

WHEREAS the reality of the actual world imposes on us, in a very urgent way, to adopt as ours the divine concern for the salvation of man according to his eternal purpose and at the time in which we live;

WHEREAS we cannot remain ignorant of the fact that relationships between mission organizations and churches that, seeking common objectives and working in common fields of labor, at times evidence lack of mutual understanding;

WE DECLARE that our relationships as the National Presbyterian Church of Mexico with churches and missionary entities will be governed by the following

PRINCIPLES

1. Autonomy. We acknowledge that the Holy Spirit, in his sovereignty, has incorporated into the Church those of us who evidence a wise variety of ministries, abilities and methods of work in the spread of the Gospel. From this it is inferred that it is He who has also bestowed on us a self-identity that demands mutual respect, understanding and complementation in the tasks He has entrusted to us. Therefore, we respect other churches and missionary entities and, by the same token, we ask for respect of the particular expression of our understanding of Biblical doctrine and the execution of our task as well as the culture and idiosyncrasy of our Country.

-3-

2. Interdependence. It is evident that the task of evangelization of our own country and the whole world cannot be undertaken either by isolated efforts or by exclusive ministries. The need is imposed on everyone of us to enter into a spirit of true interdependence that will make wise use of our particular gifts and the resources within our reach. We cannot ignore that there are at least three ways in which this interdependence is to be practiced that is:

(1) IN PARALLEL FORM, when two entities recognize their own identity and they work in a parallel form, joining ▆▆▆▆ efforts occasionally in short term projects and tasks.

(2) IN MUTUAL RESPECT, when two entities acknowledge the presence of each other and they establish relations of reciprocity and inter-change, but in complete respect of the personality, the territorial rights and the methods of work of each other, having joint labors in just a few occasions.

(3) IN COMPLETE FUSION, where such identification of purposes, efforts, objectives and ideals is reached that there exist no distinctions between a church as such and a missionary entity of a different origin from the other. As the National Presbyterian Church of Mexico we believe that the biblical imperative calls us to establish relations by the Holy Spirit, with no loss of our identify and inherent rights.

We wish above all to express a mutual submission to the lordship of Christ as Head of the Church, to our Heavenly Father as the One who issued the eternal plan of salvation of men and to the Holy Spirit as infallible Guide of the Church according to the clear guidelines of his HOly Word.

AREAS OF WORK

At the beginning of a new period of relations between the National Presbyterian Church of Mexico, the cooperating churches and missionary entities, it is to be understood that the Church of Mexico has opportunities to accomplish its ministry in different areas of work which it will perform according to its possibilities.

We suggest that these areas of work be governed according to the following order of priorities:

IN MEXICO

NEW FIELDS - It is understood as new fields those states within our country where at the present there is no Presbyterian work under the jurisdiction of the General Assembly of the National Presbyterian Church of Mexico, or that it does exist in a token form, such as:

NEW FIELDS OF THE PACIFIC AND THE NORTHWEST, that comprises the states of Baja California Norte, Baja California Sur, Colimna, Chihuahua, Durango, Nayarit, Sinaloa, and Sonora.

-4-

NEW FIELDS IN THE CENTER, that comprises the states of Aguascalientes, Guanajuato, Hidalgo, Jalisco, Puebla, Queretaro, San Luis Potosi y Tlaxcala.

The foregoing implies that there will be a difference in time in the fullfilment of the projects. Nevertheless, in both situations there will be frequent evaluation by the Committee of Joint Mission. These fields should be under the jurisdiction of the General Assembly until such a time as they can be under the jurisdiction of the presbyteries nearest to them, with the direct help of the General Assembly.

ALREADY ESTABLISHED WORK – We consider as already established work those places where both Synods and Presbyteries under the jurisdiction of the General Assembly of the National Presbyterian Church of Mexico are already working. We urge the Assembly to continue responding to its own needs and projects creating a sense of unity and cooperation within its own field of action, in general as regards its own organizations and institution, and that only in very special cases any aid from the cooperating churches be used, after previous study and after it has been approved by the General Assembly.

IN OTHER COUNTRIES –

The National Presbyterian Church of Mexico in cooperation with the churches and missionary entities, will participate in specific projects within their own geographical areas that can be accomplished such as in border areas, work among Spanish-speaking people, interchange in work or study caravans that will serve the purpose of enriching fraternal relationships, as well as other projects; also it offers, in the spirit of Christ, aid in the personnel and finances in appropriate proportion in mission projects where the Gospel needs to be preached.

JURISDICTION OF PERSONNEL

All personnel working in any project approved by the participating churches and missionary entities will be subject to the Church which received him or her according to its own structure, with the apropiate information to the church or missionary entity which sent him or her. This applies both to personnel which is already working in both countries as well as that which will participate in a project in the future. For that purpose, both parties will establish an adequate proportion.

Concerning personnel which could come to our country, it will be subject to our particular circumstances and he will be tested to verify the purity of his doctrine at least every four years, studies will be realized to try to increase national personnel and to decrease the participation of cooperating churches.

FINANCES

The same system as above will be followed in connection with financial aid for approved projects.

-5-

CONDITIONS OF OPERATION

In order to carry out this new relationship in mission between the National Presbyterian Church of Mexico and the churches and missionary entities, it is recommended:

I. That a Committee of Joint Mission be established. This Committee will be made up by the Executive Committee of the General Assembly of the National Presbyterian Church of Mexico plus the directors of the departments of Program and Development of same and those of the Synods.

II. This Committee of Joint Mission will have the following responsibilities, subject to study for ratification or rectification, as the case may be, by the respective bodies:

1. To coordinate the implementation of the plans in the areas previously specified.

2. To process projects already approved by the respective churches.

3. To test the persons coming to verify the purity of his/her doctrine.

4. To aid the bodies and/or institutions, where the missionaries have been assigned in the supervision, orientation, and pastoral care of personnel.

5. To evaluate periodically the projects approved by the cooperating churches to seek and increase National participation in personnel and financially.

6. To inform the results of the previous evaluations to the respective bodies.

7. To serve as a channel to process requests to participate in projects outside of Mexico.

PERIOD OF OPERATION

It is recommended that during this new relationship in Mission, the National Presbyterian Church of Mexico make periodic evaluations with the purpose of acquiring major responsibilities in the projects in which she is involved.

POLICY OF THE NATIONAL PRESBYTERIAN CHURCH OF MEXICO WITH REGARD TO PARA-ECCLESIASTIC MISSIONARY ENTITIES

In the face of the fact of the presence of para-ecclesiastic missionary entities which for a long or short time have worked in Mexico and which in many occasions have had a close relationship with churches, organizations and ecclesiastic bodies both officially and non-officially and which in some cases their presence is questionable, the National Presbyterian Church of Mexico establishes its policy toward those para-ecclesiastic missionary entities and/or "Faith Missions"; and because they represent missionary structures different from those which are related to a church or a denomination, it is imperative that the National Presbyterian Church of Mexico:

-6-

1. Know who those missionary entities are.

2. Know their purposes, structure in particular, administrative policy, doctrinal statements and specific objectives.

3. Regulate the participation of those missionary entities and/or "Faith Missions", especially those which might be working in the area of work of the General Assembly.

4. Show in a concrete form its disposition, if it is necessary, to enter into joint planning of common ministries and labors in order to fulfill the divine purposes for our country in a spirit of mutuality and without engaging in any competition whatsoever.

In order to reach these objectives it is recommended that both parties be willing to enter into serious conversations in order to determine the fields of mutual action, the duties and privileges that both parties will acquire, the length of specific projects, the standards of periodic evaluation that should be applied both to the relationship and to the projects, and all of those details that might be relevant for each particular missionary entity, according to its own individual circumstances.

The National Presbyterian Church of Mexico reserves the right to establish or not establish relationships with those entities, providing the appropriate information to the ecclesiastical bodies under its jurisdiction.

This document was approved by the General Assembly of the National Presbyterian Church of Mexico in its XIV special called meeting of July 10-13, 1979 in the Filadelfia Church of Guernavacas, Morelos.

The Secretary:

Pbro. Juan Garcia Martinez

THE COMMITTEE:

Pbro. Samuel Trinidad B., Dr. Pablo Perez Morales, Pbro. Juan Garcia Martinez, Pbro. Isaias Uc Colli, Dr. Alberto Alvarado B., Dr. Saul Tijerina Gonzalez, Pbro. Severo Ek. Profr. David Macias S.

Appendix B (See next pages)

PRESBYTERIAN BORDER MINISTRY
PROGRAM HISTORY, GOALS AND ORGANIZATION

Introduction

The U.S. door to all of Latin America begins geographically at the U.S./Mexico border. But the cultural border with Latin American actually begins far north of the border - within the U.S. Americans eat at Mexican and Caribbean restaurants, can watch television in Spanish, read bilingual advertisements and information signs, and in many states can vote in either English or Spanish. Many of the largest employers in Mexico are U.S. companies, located primarily in border communities. Likewise, the Dallas Cowboys are a regularly part of every Mexican's Sunday TV diet. We are neighbors with an increasingly blurred border.

As the physical border is increasingly militarized by the U.S., it becomes a symbolic battle front. Each nation blames the other for their inability to deal effectively with domestic issues. The list of the neighbor's sins includes the U.S. blaming Mexico for undocumented immigration, and Mexico blaming its drug trafficking problems on the U.S. market for illegal drugs.

The Bible reminds us that what we sow will be reaped by our children's children. If U.S. and Mexican Presbyterians sow seeds of understanding and cooperation today, there is hope that our grandchildren will break down the walls of separation and learn to live as neighbors. (Eph. 2:14)

The Presbyterian Church (USA) and the National Presbyterian Church of Mexico have covenanted to begin the process of living and working as neighbors. We have promised to behave towards one another as citizens of the Kingdom of God, and thereby witness to a power that transcends cultural and national loyalties.

The presence of seven mission sites has provided Presbyterian Border Ministry with a unique opportunity to offer a challenge to U.S. and Mexican churches. Because of the proximity of the border, churches have discovered international mission in their "back yards." To be able to provide Christians with a hands on experience gives them a new understanding of, and appreciation for, the mission of the Church.

I. 1962-1999

In 1962, as the National Presbyterian Church of Mexico began planning for its centennial in 1972, it invited the United Presbyterian Church (USA) and the Presbyterian Church in the U.S. to enter into a 10 year moratorium. It was mutually agreed that beginning in 1962 missionary terms would not be renewed, that over a 10 year period all missionaries would be withdrawn, and the NPCM would ultimately become totally self-supporting, self-governing and self-propagating.

In 1979, the general assemblies of the two churches, meeting in Kansas City, received an invitation from the National Presbyterian Church of Mexico to consider renewing their mission partnership. The new covenant was ratified by all three churches in 1980.

The invitation, entitled "A New Relation in Joint Mission," established the objectives for joint mission as well as the standards that would govern the new partnership. Several principles of collaboration were spelled out: that "a wise use be made of the particular gifts and the resources at our disposal"; that we would "express our mutual obedience to the Lordship of Jesus Christ as Head of the Church, to our Heavenly Father, the source of the eternal plan for the salvation of humankind, and to the Holy Spirit as the unfailing guide of the Church, as given by clear directions in scripture."

When the new document was adopted, the Joint Mission Commission (JMC) was created. This new body was made up of general assembly and synod representatives of both national churches.

As this new relationship was being forged, the U.S. church had two couples in training for mission sites in Tepic and Colima, Mexico. When changes in Mexican immigration policy made it impossible for them to take up residence in these locations, they were invited by the JMC to consider the border as their mission field. Reassignments were made to the Tijuana/San Diego area, which is known today as "Pueblos Hermanos", and to the Agua Prieta/Douglas, AZ, area, which is now "Frontera de Cristo".

In 1984 the JMC created the Binational Border Committee to oversee the work of Presbyterian Border Ministry(PBM). The JMC named representatives to the committee and authorized naming 2 binational coordinators to oversee the work of the expanding ministry.

Between 1985 and 1992, the following new ministries were started: "Project Amistad", Piedras Negras/Eagle Pass (1985), "Laredos Unidos", Nuevo Laredo/Laredo (1988), and "Programa Nogalhillos", Nogales, Sonora/Nogales, Arizona (1992). In 1989, "Project Verdad", El Paso/Juarez, was officially closed as a binational ministry. Ministry, however, continued on both sides of the border. Under the jurisdiction of Tres Rios Presbytery(PCUSA), and a new name, "Project Vida" continued ministry in El Paso, Texas. Under the jurisdiction of the JMC, and the name "Paso del Norte", ministry was continued in Juarez, Chihuahua, Mexico.

In 1986 the JMC approved the creation of the Presbyterian Border Ministry Corporation. Established under Texas law it was charged with promoting financial support for the work of PBM. The Corporation was made accountable to the JMC.

In October of 1989 a consultation was called by the JMC in Mexico City. The ministry was evaluated and after careful analysis the following changes were approved:

- Representation on the Binational Border Committee would come from those presbyteries where border ministries were located.
- The Binational Border Committee was reconstituted to include 7 representatives from each side of the border(14 in total), representing border synods, presbyteries and general assemblies.

In April of 1990, at the regular meeting held in Laredo, TX, the Border Committee approved a comprehensive set of goals and objectives to guide the work of Presbyterian Border Ministry. It continues to guide program development for each of the 7 ministries. (See Goals and Objectives section II)

In 1993 the JMC once again set in motion an extensive evaluation process to determine the effectiveness of the ministry and the existing administrative structure. A survey was conducted, two special forums were held in which participants from all of the border presbyteries, synods and general assemblies, participated.

Several changes were proposed. On Nov. 8, 1995, the JMC approved recommendations for creating a new administrative entity - to be called the Presbyterian Border Ministry Council. The Council was authorized to draw up by-laws and convene its first meeting, which was held April 29-30, 1996 in El Paso, TX.

The Council retained the number of representatives of its predecessor (7+7 or 14). Representation from Mexico is composed of one representative from each of the 4 border presbyteries where ministry is conducted, one from each of its two border synods, and one representative elected by the General Assembly. U.S. representation is elected by 6 border presbyteries, plus one elected by the General Assembly Council. Both general assemblies send one non-voting staff person.

Finally, in May of 1998, with the blessing of the Presbyterian Border Ministry Council, the U.S. Presbyteries of Tres Rios and Sierra Blanca, and the Mexican Presbytery of the Northwest, agreed to reconstitute a binational ministry between Juarez, Chihuahua and El Paso, TX. The newly formed board of directors voted to call the renewed binational ministry "Pasos de Fe."

II. Presbyterian Border Ministry Goals and Objectives

The following is a brief outline of the basic principles that guide program development and the administration of PBM. Although it envisions a binational ministry with new church development and redevelopment work with churches on both sides of the border, the development of new churches and ministries of compassion (goals 1 &2), have been conducted almost exclusively in Mexico. Likewise goal 3, intended to draw churches from both nations into mission on the border, has been almost exclusively a program for U.S. churches.

A. MISSION STATEMENT

Presbyterian Border Ministry is a joint labor of the Presbyterian Churches of the U.S. and Mexico. It is called to share a holistic gospel with those who live along the 2,000 mile U.S./Mexican border, by responding to their spiritual, emotional, physical, and material needs.

The mission of Presbyterian Border Ministry (PBM) is to proclaim and witness to the Gospel of Jesus Christ by:

1. Engaging in new church development with the presbytery of jurisdiction.
2. Engaging in ministries of compassion which empower people and communities.

3. Promoting mission education by providing opportunities for U.S. and Mexican Presbyterians to directly experience the work of Presbyterian Border Ministry.
4. Promoting mutuality in mission through binational structures for oversight and implementation of the ministry.
5. Collaborating with and supporting existing border churches.

B. THEOLOGICAL AFFIRMATIONS

The Kingdom of God includes all creation (Rom. 8:21; Eph. 1:9-10). It has no boundaries, so as called servants of the Christ we dare not allow borders to divide our mission.

The Presbyterian Border Ministry Council has adopted 3 basic theological affirmations. They guide all present and future mission efforts. These affirmations are expressed in the following manner:

1. We must be partners in mission. The nature of the Kingdom is such that it transcends nationalities and cultural differences. The Kingdom has been announced by the God of all nations, who gave his Son in order to bring reconciliation between all human beings and between them and their Creator. We witness to the reconciling power of the Gospel when we do mission together.

2. We must be partners in the common task of strengthening the Church. We owe our identity to the Church. We are heirs of a rich legacy that the Church has faithfully kept for us. the Gospel. It is the Church that will bless our labors and keep them for posterity.

3. We have been called to proclaim all the Gospel for everyone in both word and deed. For the Gospel to have validity it must be expressed in terms of the needs that people have, as they themselves perceive those needs.

C. PRESBYTERIAN BORDER MINISTRY: NEEDS, VISION AND PLAN

The needs of people living on the border are unique, yet common. They need to be part of a community with hope and vision which affirms and values them. They need the strength to face each day that only God can provide. They need adequate food, health care, clean water, sanitation, jobs, housing, and healthy recreational opportunities. An outline of operational guidelines for Presbyterian Border Ministry is presented in the following form:

CHURCH DEVELOPMENT

NEED: The border is an impersonal and fragmented community. Residents need skills and hope to face unique challenges and a vision of community where their personal needs and those of the larger community are seen as interdependent.

VISION: The creation of Christian communities capable of giving dignity and vision to individuals and communities who live in the shadow of the border.

4

PLAN:

1. NEW CHURCH DEVELOPMENT
Encourage each organized church to sponsor a new mission.

2. EVANGELISM
Promote and implement training programs for effective evangelism on the border for pastors and appropriate program staff.

3. DEVELOPMENT OF A COMPREHENSIVE CHURCH EDUCATION PROGRAM
Develop and promote Christian education materials in Spanish and English, appropriate to the border context.

4. DEVELOPMENT OF A COMPREHENSIVE STEWARDSHIP PROGRAM
Equip congregations on the border to achieve financial independence.

5. DEVELOPMENT OF YOUTH, WOMEN AND MEN'S PROGRAMS
Develop groups at all established congregations.

6. DEVELOPMENT OF OFFICER TRAINING PROGRAMS
Identify and train local leadership for all congregations.

7. DEVELOPMENT OF A PLAN FOR LOCAL CHURCHES TO OVERSEE COMMUNITY HEALTH, EDUCATION AND ECONOMIC AND COMMUNITY DEVELOPMENT PROGRAMS
Assist and encourage local congregations to take ever increasing responsibility for community outreach and service programs.

COMMUNITY HEALTH

NEED: Chronic undernourishment and illness are facts of life for thousands of residents in marginal border communities. The mortality rate for infants exceeds World Health Organization standards. Medical attention is often sought by the poor only in emergencies.

VISION: That the Church be a servant community, providing health services as a practical expression of God's love for the world.

PLAN:

1. DEVELOPMENT OF PRIMARY CARE CLINICS
Offer primary health clinic services (curative and preventative) in marginal communities.

2. HEALTH EDUCATION PROGRAMS
Offer health promoter programs to provide communities with indigenous health advocates.

5

3. CHILDREN'S DAILY NUTRITION PROGRAM
Provide children's nutrition programs at targeted Presbyterian Border Ministry sites.

4. POTABLE WATER PROCUREMENT AND SANITATION
Promote and implement programs for the procurement of potable water and sanitation facilities.

COMMUNITY EDUCATION

NEED: Children need preschool education and day care; adults need basic education and training opportunities.

VISION: That preschool children be prepared for formal education, and adult literacy and vocational training programs be established for job readiness.

PLAN:

1. PRE-SCHOOL EDUCATION
Promote preschool programs where needed.

2. VOCATIONAL TRAINING, LITERACY, AND TUTORING
Promote adult education opportunities where feasible.

ECONOMIC AND COMMUNITY DEVELOPMENT

NEED: Basic needs have far outstripped each Mexican border city's ability to deliver. Unemployment is high, housing is inadequate and healthy recreational opportunities are scarce.

VISION: Leadership with adequate skills to take greater control of their community's destiny.

PLAN:

1. SMALL BUSINESS DEVELOPMENT
Encourage support for small business development at Presbyterian Border Ministry sites.

2. COMMUNITY DEVELOPMENT
Promote programs which develop skills necessary to be productive citizens.

3. RECREATION PROGRAMS
Promote healthy recreational programs at border sites.

CREATION OF SUPPORT STRUCTURES TO ENABLE EFFECTIVE MINISTRY

NEED: Presbyterian Border Ministry is unique by virtue of its location. It is bicultural and binational, its context is the longest border in the world where a developed nation and a developing nation meet. It is a ministry where two churches have covenanted to be in mission together. It is a ministry which, by its very nature, requires extraordinary flexibility and patience of those who accept the challenge.

VISION: That those called to mission on the border be equipped for the task.

PLAN:

1. Promote and implement ongoing national and regional training programs for all ministry staff.

2. Promote and implement regular intercultural training events for board members at each local project.

3. Develop a comprehensive information network for Presbyterian Border Ministry sites.

PROVIDING OPPORTUNITIES FOR MISSION EDUCATION

NEED: Worldwide mission is mandated by every New Testament Writer. A significant portion of the Presbyterian Church (USA) and the National Presbyterian Church of Mexico have not responded to Christ's call to mission.

VISION: That Presbyterian Border Ministry provide opportunities for Presbyterians to participate in worldwide mission.

PLAN:

1. Develop and promote a comprehensive program for all mission teams planning to participate in a cross cultural mission experience.

2. Produce curriculum materials that prepare groups for an immersion experience that helps them internalize the experience while on site, helps them reflect on the experience in the context of their own personal faith journey, and helps them discover ways to share their mission learnings back home.

3. The design of a comprehensive short term mission experiences for the Presbyterian Church (USA) should be guided by the following mission statement:

7

MISSION STATEMENT

Seeking to be faithful to Christ's call, Presbyterian Border Ministry offers a work study experience which provides an opportunity for members of a mission team to:

1. participate in worldwide mission;
2. observe and appreciate how the PC(USA) and the National Presbyterian Church of Mexico engage in mutual mission;
3. identify and value the gifts of partners in ministry;
4. see through another's eyes the impact of U.S. and Mexican lifestyles on neighbors;
5. vitalize the faith of individuals and faith communities by sharing and interpreting the experience.

III. Funding

The World Wide Ministries Division(WWMD) of the Presbyterian Church (USA) funds the U.S. Coordinator and the mission personnel at ministry sites. Funding for the Presbyterian Border Ministry Council, its operation and staff, as well as the operation of the Corporation is secured by the Presbyterian Border Ministry Corporation. Primary responsibility for program funding of local ministry, although supported by the PBM Council and Corporation, remains with the ministry itself.

IV. ADMINISTRATIVE PRINCIPLES, GUIDELINES AND STRUCTURE

Presbyterian Border Ministry is one ministry with multiple sites. Each project has developed staffing patterns which respond to its program goals. Ministries have tended to deploy project leadership from Mexico in areas of evangelism and church development, and U.S. leadership in areas of community development and administration. The philosophy of Presbyterian Border Ministry calls for a team approach where tasks assignments are subject to needs and skills which each team member brings to the project. Assignment of duties, which falls under the heading of job descriptions, is the direct responsibility of the local board.

The local administrative body is the board of directors, with equal representation from local presbyteries from each national church. The project leadership team, with the oversight of the Board, has responsibility for planning, developing, and coordinating all project activities. They are responsible for evaluating and assessing the needs and resources of the area to be served by the project, and determining and recommending the programs that are both feasible and desirable

The desired administrative model continues to be one that is faithful to the intent of the covenant between our respective national churches. It is one which is always being reformed to better reflect our desire to be a shared binational team ministry. As the model evolves, hopefully more adequate terminology will be discovered to describe the nature and mission of Presbyterian Border Ministry.

(For a visual understanding of the structure of PBM see the attached organizational chart)

1/15/99 - Jerry Stacy

Presbyterian Border Region Outreach

... Living out the Gospel of Jesus Christ holistically on both sides of the US-Mexico Border, in partnership with other faith organizations and nonprofits to reduce poverty and violence in the Border Region

March 1, 2013

1. Definition of Our Mission and Purpose

PBM is an umbrella for ministry sites to help facilitate our holistic approach to addressing root causes of poverty and promoting reconciliation in cultures of violence.

In all our work we are accountable first to our Lord Jesus Christ, and through His Spirit to one another, always responding to God's image in our neighbor.

PBRO will conduct an annual program and external financial audit.

2. Staffing

a. PBRO Facilitator
Job description: Fulltime co mission worker through PCUSA World Mission with three month pre-assignment itineration/training before they arrive on-site. This person will be accountable to PBRO board who will supervise him/her.

Requirements/Qualifications
- Person of deep faith rooted in church life
- Bilingual (English/Spanish)
- US citizen or person with current visa to work in the US
- Good interpersonal skills (individuals and groups)
- Heavy travel requirements
- Previous experience (Latin America and/or border preferred)
- Cultural understanding
- Theological training/knowledge
- Community development and urban ministry knowledge
- Team worker
- Self starter
- Communication experience and skill
- Located in El Paso
- Must visit each site at least 3 times annually and at least 3 PCUSA presbytery or supporting church visits in the site areas
- Update website, newsletter, Facebook, other means of communication
- Will be responsible for organizing at least one annual physical gathering and four virtual gatherings with all sites participating to celebrate, educate, equip, support, provide theological reflection, and conduct business.

Cost: $80,000 + $10,000 travel with PBRO providing $60,000

b. Transitional Support Staff
Present Funds Development Coordinator will be given two months notice (end date of April 30, 2013)

10 hour a week office assistant position will be created. This temporary position will be

1

located in El Paso beginning April 1, 2013.

This position includes bookkeeping, logistical support of meetings and technical assistance with funding letters, website and other forms of communication. Salary: $14 per hour with $30 a week towards health insurance.

A period of orientation will be conducted by the present Funds Development Coordinator, to include an on-site meeting. All files and equipment will be transferred to the El Paso site.

Three months after the facilitator begins onsite service, this temporary position will be reevaluated.

3. Participatory Evaluations

With staff person, each ministry site needs to continue the participatory evaluation and define its goals and its partners (churches, NGOs):

a. Facilitator will facilitate examination of the resources and needs of the ministry sites and their communities, as they relate to poverty and violence.
b. Facilitator will report to the PBRO board, who will in turn provide regular feedback and suggestions.
c. Each ministry site will continue to be involved in its own follow-up to these evaluations. Each site will explore the issues facing its communities, identify its strengths, what resources or base of support it has to fulfill its mission.

4. The Need for Research

In year one, facilitator and local boards will pursue the following:

a. What information is available that details specific types of violence and areas of poverty along the border, and where do they occur? Such a geographic identification allows us to specifically target areas of need. Such an assessment may already be available -- it is a customary step in building responses to a wide variety of concerns. The process is not so different than churches reviewing population data before recommending a new church plant in a neighborhood, or a pastor nominating committee doing a Mission Study.
b. What other organizations, faith based, non-faith based, NGO's, public organizations, community development programs, etc., exist in the Project's area at the present time? Which appear willing to partner with PBM in a variety of actions and faith initiatives? Each community will have different sets of folks active on the front lines -- and determining who they are before going in to seek information and direction would avoid wasting time.
c. Treating the root of poverty and violence revolves around reconciliation and holistic

2

renewal through Jesus Christ. INPM will continue to build churches and PBRO can introduce people to INPM churches and/or other local churches in the course of its work.

d. Is there a representative group of people who exist in the targeted areas of need that could be interviewed and whose perceptions included in the analysis? These could be people of faith, and/or community members completely separate from churches.

5. PBRO, in conjunction with facilitator and local ministry sites will:

- Enlist existing ministry site boards to join in implementing the new mission
- Enlist existing PCUSA Mission co-workers
- "Re-Introduce" PBM as PBRO within PCUSA, Synods, Presbyteries, and churches
- Submit Articles about PBRO to Presbyterian Missions publications, others
- Appeal to Current Donor Base for Funds; Expand to Potential New Donors
- Research, Identify, Develop Relationships and Come Alongside Existing Social Service Agencies in the Border Region who Share our Mission
- Encourage/Recruit US Churches to Donate, to Visit, to Work with these Agencies
- Prepare information packets for visiting groups and partners
- Facilitator will ensure Line 202 must have $20,000 in it (funding to ministry sites)